Thomas Shadwell

By MICHAEL W. ALSSID

Boston University

Twayne Publishers, Inc.   ::   New York

To Rebecca

Preface

APART from Albert S. Borgman's study of Thomas Shadwell and Montague Summers' lengthy introduction to the standard edition of his works, Shadwell has been no doubt the most neglected of the important Restoration dramatists. Both of these critics, particularly the latter, attempted to restore their subject to a position of prominence; but their studies, written some forty years ago, concentrate heavily upon biographical matters and sources and, only in a superficial way, do they show—as I wish with greater thoroughness to show in this first book-length critical study—how highly conscious an artist Shadwell was and how intelligently and perceptively he translated into his plays many of the profound and ironic views of man, society, and art which he and his age held.

The critical neglect of Shadwell is largely a result of the assumption that excellence in Restoration comedy is available chiefly in the works of men like Etherege, Wycherley, and Congreve—and chiefly in their masterpieces. Shadwell is considered dispensable because, among other things, he did not produce plays which display the kind of wit which we associate with these artists. Yet revaluations of the author of *The Squire of Alsatia* and *Bury-Fair* must begin with an awareness that he was not, except in certain ways, trying to write plays like theirs. His temperament, his views of life and art, his style—in short, his artistic talent—were bolder, more hammer-like in their satiric blows, less sophisticated than theirs. There is a Swiftian texture in Shadwell's thought and style, a kind of "peevish" cynicism which disapproves of excessive refinement, a vivid recognition of the animalistic nature of man which underlies the uncompromising satiric vision of all of his plays and of many of his poems. Only ironically does he relieve the harshness of his satire. Through irony he shows us how to accept and perhaps to sympathize with the fools and the occasional wise men and women of his plays. To understand the importance of Shadwell, we must broaden our concept of Restoration comedy so as to allow for his more brutally relentless portraits of human nature, portraits rarely subsumed under the witty style of the comedies of the period which have been called (and quite rightly) "the best."

My primary purpose is to indicate the complexity that informs Shadwell's art. I present his works in the form of "readings" which may be independently studied for particular plays but which, as a group, are intended to show the nature and importance of his contribution to the drama of his time. In Chapter 1, after briefly outlining his career, I discuss his comic theory and his concept of comic heroes, heroines, and fools. The next three chapters are devoted to eight of his comedies: Chapter 2, to the first three as they illustrate various recurrent features of his comic vision; Chapter 3, to what has been called his single attempt at "wit" comedy (*Epsom-Wells*) and to what is perhaps his most vigorous "humors" satire (*The Virtuoso*); and Chapter 4, to three plays which form a unit that highlights his persistent concern with the place of women in a comic world. Chapters 5 and 6 are devoted to the two most neglected areas in Shadwell, his efforts in pastoral, opera and tragedy, and his poetry. Chapters 7 and 8 consider the five comedies written after his period of silence. These comedies show not the slightest weakening of his dramatic skill and verve; but their satiric textures are more mellow suggesting that he grew in his later years increasingly conscious of his role of public "servant" who could voice, as William and Mary's laureate, long held ideals of a limited monarchial system. Chapter 9 contains a brief consideration of his place in Restoration drama.

MICHAEL W. ALSSID

Boston University

Contents

Chronology

1641 or Birth of Thomas Shadwell at Santon Hall, parish of
1642   Santon, Norfolk.

1654   After five years of tutoring at home, Shadwell enters the
       King Edward VI Free Grammar School, Bury St. Ed-
       munds.

1656   Admitted to Gonville and Caius College, Cambridge
       (December 17), but left sometime after without taking
       a degree.

1658   Enters Middle Temple to study law (July 7). Sometime
       during the decade (1658-1668) was clerk to Sir Robert
       Long, Auditor of the Exchequer.

1664 or Spends four months in Ireland. May have traveled on
1665   Continent.

1663-   (c.) Marries Anne Gibbs, formerly the wife of Thomas
1667   Gaudy or Gawdy.

1668   *The Sullen Lovers,* his first comedy, successfully pro-
       duced at Lincoln Inn's Fields.

1668/9 *The Royal Shepherdess,* a pastoral tragi-comedy, pro-
       duced at Lincoln Inn's Fields.

1670   *The Humorists,* a comedy, produced at Lincoln Inn's
       Fields.

1671   *The Hypocrite,* an unpublished comedy probably pro-
       duced. Shadwell stays at Chadderton Hall, near Old-
       ham (April-May). Birth of his first son, John, prob-
       ably in this year.

1671/2 *The Miser,* a comedy anonymously produced at the
       Theatre Royal in Bridges Street.

1672   *Epsom-Wells,* a comedy, produced at Dorset Garden.

1673/4 Record (January 20), of baptism of son, George.

1674   Operatic version of *The Tempest,* produced at Dorset
       Garden.

1674/5   *Psyche,* an opera, produced at Dorset Garden.

1675   *The Libertine,* a tragedy, produced at Dorset Garden.

1676   *The Virtuoso,* a comedy, produced at Dorset Garden.

1677/8   Adaptation of Shakespeare's *Timon of Athens* produced at Dorset Garden. Record (February 21), burial of son, George.

1678   *A True Widow,* a comedy, produced at Dorset Garden.

1679   *The Woman-Captain,* a comedy, produced at Dorset Garden.

1680   Record (September 21), christening of son, William.

1681   After various delays, the politically and religiously controversial comedy, *The Lancashire Witches* (at Dorset Garden), the last of the plays to be staged before 1668.

1682   Satire, *The Medal of John Bayes* published.

1683   *Some Reflections Upon the Pretended Parallel,* a criticism of Dryden's *The Duke of Guise,* published; probably written in collaboration with Settle and Thomas Hunt.

1686   Record (October 27), burial of William and christening of daughter, Anne.

1687   *The Tenth Satyr of Juvenal,* a translation with notes, published. Resides perhaps at Copt-Hall, the Earl of Dorset's estate.

1688   *The Squire of Alsatia,* a comedy, produced at the Theatre Royal in Drury Lane.

1688/9   Warrant swearing Shadwell into his post as Poet Laureate (March 9).

1689   *Bury-Fair,* a comedy, produced at the Theatre Royal in Drury Lane; at about the same time (April 30) in which the first of his official odes (for the birthday of Queen Mary), performed with music by Purcell. Patent confirming his position as Laureate and Historiographer Royal drawn up (August 29).

1690   *The Amorous Bigotte* and *The Scowrers,* two comedies, produced at the Theatre Royal in Drury Lane.

1692   Death of Shadwell (November 19 or 20); burial at St. Luke's Chelsea Parish Church (November 24). *The*

Volunteers, his last comedy, posthumously produced at the Theatre Royal in Drury Lane.

1715   His eldest son John, royal physician, knighted by Queen Anne.

1720   Collected edition of Shadwell's plays, in four volumes, probably supervised by Sir John Shadwell.

1726   Death of a son, Charles (August 12 in Dublin), author of a successful comedy *The Fair Quaker of Deal; or, The Humours of the Navy* (1710).

Thomas Shadwell

CHAPTER 1

'Born to Expose the Follies of the Age'

FEW facts of Shadwell's life have been preserved and most of them are fragmentary and uncertain.[1] He was born sometime between 1640 and 1642, probably at Santon Hall in Norfolk of an old Staffordshire family. His father John Shadwell, a man wealthy by inheritance and loyal to Charles I during the turbulent civil wars, encouraged his son's intellectual and artistic development by hiring a tutor (a Mr. Roberts) and a musical instructor (John Jenkins) before Thomas was sent to the King Edward VI Free Grammar School at Bury St. Edmunds. There under the headmaster Thomas Stephens, Thomas acquired his basic knowledge of Classical languages; and, years later, he used the Bury setting for his finest satire on country life, *Bury-Fair*. On December 17, 1656, he entered Gonville and Caius College, Cambridge, as a pensioner to the bachelor's table. Without having received a degree from Cambridge, he was admitted, some nineteen months later on July 7, 1658, to the Middle Temple in pursuit of a career in law. He may perhaps have traveled abroad in the early 1660's, and he seems to have visited Ireland for four months in 1665, probably in the company of his father who was Recorder of Galway and Attorney General for Connaught.

Sometime before the successful production of his first play, *The Sullen Lovers* in 1668, Shadwell met the great seventeenth-century patron of the arts, William Cavendish, the Duke of Newcastle, "the only *Mecaenas* of our Age," at the Duke's estate at Welbeck.[2] Their meeting was a crucial one: the Duke appears not only to have given him favors but to have encouraged him to embark upon a career as dramatist. Even more important, the Duke, who had been Ben Jonson's patron and friend, may have stimulated Shadwell's interest in the particular *kind* of comedy, Jonsonian "humors" comedy, of which Shadwell was to become the chief exponent during the Restoration. For young Shadwell,

a "Son of Ben," the Duke represented no doubt a living link between Jonson and himself. Shadwell's relationship with the
Cavendish family is, in part, recorded in his various dedications
to the Duke and his family. These brief adulatory pieces—together with poems and dedications to such men as Wycherley,
Dorset, Buckingham, and Sedley—give some indication of his
familiarity with the great wits and patrons of the age whose
libertinism he made the philosophic basis of the characters and
actions of his dramatic heroes.[3] How familiar he was with these
men remains, however, conjectural.

Between 1663 and 1667, Shadwell married Anne Gibbs, a
talented actress in the Duke's Company who played the
atrabilious Emilia in *The Sullen Lovers* and who continued to
act comic and tragic roles throughout the 1670's when her husband was reaching the peak of his reputation as a new voice in
the theater.[4] The *éclat* of his first comedy is often attributed to
its scathing satire of living persons; and, although Shadwell was
pleased with the reception of the play, he took pains to prevent
the impression that he sought merely popular success. In his
Preface to *The Sullen Lovers*, he insisted upon the esthetic
significance of his play, declaring himself a disciple of Jonson
and taking a firm stand against the new Restoration comedy of
manners or wit which men like Dryden were championing.
Shadwell's critical observations on the nature of true comedy,
"humors" comedy, inaugurated a brief but significant literary
skirmish between him and the elder dramatist. It was significant
because Shadwell, in attacking modern wit comedy and in de-
fending the older "humors" comedy, stated the crucial characteristics of his comic theory: its moral-philosophical implications,
its relationship to satire, and its great concern for characterization. His major remarks appeared in the prefaces to his next two
plays, the pastoral tragi-comedy *The Royal Shepherdess* of
1668/9, and *The Humorists* of 1670, a comedy which, as its
title implies, may have been intended as an example *par excellence* of "humors" comedy.

The Dryden-Shadwell disputes over what constituted true
comedy for a modern audience subsided after the publication of
The Humorists, and by 1674 the two writers were apparently
on friendly terms. In that year appeared the anonymous *Notes
and Observations On the Empress of Morocco*, a critical attack

on Elkanah Settle in which Shadwell and Dryden collaborated with John Crowne. Apart from *Epsom-Wells* and *The Virtuoso,* Shadwell devoted his time between 1671 and 1678 to five adaptations of French and English plays, among them Molière's *L'Avare* and Shakespeare's *Timon of Athens.* These adaptations, in particular two operas *The Tempest* and *Psyche,* were highly successful; indeed, they proved more profitable financially than did Shadwell's "humors" comedies which, as he often remarked, were far more difficult to write. Yet after *Timon* he returned to his favorite mode and between 1678 and 1681 wrote three comedies which may accurately be described as his "feminist" plays, since all three of them celebrate in different ways the genius of women: *A True Widow,* for which Dryden wrote the Prologue; *The Woman-Captain,* a farcical play without a hero; and *The Lancashire Witches,* a strong satire on religion (Catholic and Anglican) produced at the height of the political struggles between Shaftesbury and the Crown for the exclusion of James from the succession. The *Witches* makes emphatic Shadwell's Whiggish political sentiments. No new plays by Shadwell were produced for seven years after the *Witches.* Like so many seventeenth-century artists, Shadwell's literary fortunes were intimately related to his political attitudes. Again, however, specific reasons for his retirement from the stage are not known.[5]

Various political satires in prose and verse written during and after 1682 have been attributed to Shadwell, but in most instances without adequate proof except for *The Medal of John Bayes,* a virulent poetic rebuttal to Dryden's attack on Shaftesbury and the Exclusionists in *The Medal.* Shadwell's satire was followed by the publication of Dryden's devastating portrait of Shadwell as the master of incompetence and dullness in *Mac Flecknoe,* and soon after by the less brilliant, less devastating portrait of Shadwell as Og in *Absalom and Achitophel, Part Two.*[6] Turning Shadwell into something of a "humors" character in *Mac Flecknoe,* Dryden stressed chiefly his enemy's failure as an artist; in Og, he derided Shadwell's obesity, his excessive drinking, his Whiggism.

These quarrels persisted when, after the appearance of the Dryden-Lee play *The Duke of Guise,* Shadwell published a prose criticism of the play (*Some Reflections on the Pretended Parallel*) in which he castigated the *"old Serpent* Bayes" as the arch political traitor in the vituperative style of *The Medal of John Bayes.* Dryden brought the quarrel to a close with his prose *Vindication,* but the verve and wit of his caricatures of Shadwell were ebbing. Like Shadwell, Dryden repeated old charges against the enemy: he was a villain-buffoon, a clumsy and drunken devil, an obvious fool.

The next five years brought severe financial hardship to Shadwell since he could not earn a living as a playwright probably for the reasons given in the Prologue to *Bury-Fair* in 1689:

> *Our* Author *then opprest, would have you know it,*
> *Was Silenc'd for a* Non-conformist *Poet:*
> *In those* hard times *he bore the utmost* test,
> *And now he Swears he's* Loyal *as the best.*

It is altogether likely that, during the period of silence, he assisted Tom Jevon in writing *The Devil is a Wife,* a farce produced in 1685/6.[7] At this time Shadwell lived in the parish of St. Bride's, for church records of October 27, 1686, list the death of a son William and the christening of a daughter Anne. By 1687, his prospects began to improve. His old patron Sir Charles Sedley assisted him financially, and he published his translation of Juvenal's Tenth Satire.

But not until 1688 did Shadwell find the opportunity to reinstate himself as a leading dramatist. In that year, *The Squire of Alsatia,* the play that broke his seven-years' silence, was performed with extraordinary success. In the Dedication to the Earl of Dorset, Shadwell tells of writing the first act in the congenial atmosphere of Copt-Hall, the Earl's estate, and it was perhaps the Earl who encouraged him to offer his talents in celebration of the arrival of William and Mary and the advent of the Bloodless Revolution.

The new political atmosphere, in which he was indeed as "Loyal *as the best,*" proved artistically productive; in the last years of his life he expressed his creative talents in two distinctly different ways: he wrote five comedies for the stage and he composed a series of panegyric poems in his official position as Poet Laureate and Royal Historiographer. The Earl of Dorset, Lord Chamberlain under William and Mary, had secured this post for Shadwell. Providing the destitute playwright with £300 and "one Butt or Pype" of canary wine a year, the post was largely a reward for Shadwell's anti-papal, exclusionist associations during the late 1670's and early 1680's. It could not have been in recognition of his poetic ability or achievement since he had written only a handful of non-dramatic poems before 1688, and these scarcely measure up to the high standards set for the laureateship by his predecessor Dryden.

Politically, Shadwell was elated with the new monarchs. His intention of praising them effectively cannot be doubted and, hence, cannot account for the generally "stale" quality of even his best laureate poems. But his forte was comedy, the satiric view of man. He never felt at home when treating the heroic themes of panegyric. He considered human nature "generically as the source of comic materials,"[8] not as the source of inflated ideations.

Shadwell was also, in the last years, troubled by poor health. In the dedications of *Bury-Fair* and *The Amorous Bigotte,* he mentioned a *"painful sickness"* which made even the composition of comedy difficult, and in the Prologue to *The Scowrers,* the last play produced during his lifetime, the audience was informed that *"He of the Gout lay in."* The final years, from 1691 until his death on November 19 or 20, 1692, were particularly difficult. He produced only two major works, *Votum Perenne* (a New Year's Day Ode for William III then engaged in his European wars) and *The Volunteers* (his last comedy, which uses these wars as its background), staged about a month after his death. It is assumed that he died of an overdose of opium to which he was addicted.

His funeral sermon was delivered by Nicholas Brady, a minister whose play, *The Rape; or, The Innocent Imposters,* Shadwell, against opposition, helped to bring to the stage shortly before he died and for which he wrote the witty Epilogue.[9] John Dennis, an admirer of Shadwell, composed a Dedication for *The Volunteers;* for reasons unknown it was replaced by a brief address to Queen Mary and signed by Shadwell's widow.[10] Thomas Durfey contributed the comic Prologue to the play: he advised the audience to brush aside *"Sad Thoughts"* of Shadwell's death and to enjoy his merry "Orphan Play." The anonymous Epilogue,

"Spoken by one in deep Mourning," celebrates with greater seriousness the ideal of comic art which Shadwell had advocated throughout his career:

> SHADWELL *the great Support oth' Comick Stage,*
> *Born to expose the Follies of the Age:*
> *To whip prevailing Vices, and unite*
> Mirth *with* Instruction, Profit *with* Delight:
> *For large Idea's and a flowing* Pen,
> *First of our* Times, *and second but to* Ben. . . .

I *The Critical Foci*

Critical estimations of Shadwell's achievement have differed considerably in and after his lifetime.[11] Never adjudging him a major dramatist, most critics have nevertheless recognized his importance in the history of dramatic literature and have offered two, perhaps three, reasons for his importance. First, he is regarded as the leading Restoration proponent of the Jonsonian "humors" tradition; secondly, as a "realistic" playwright whose works contain rich details of contemporary life, he is a quarry for social historians. The third recurrent critical motif has to do with the Dryden quarrels out of which emerged the Mac Flecknoe and Og portraits. These portraits have come to represent for many students of the Restoration the real Shadwell. Their damage to his reputation is inestimable and surely unparalleled in English literature. Dryden's mock-heroics have proved an irresistible reference to nearly every critic:

> Sh—— alone, of all my sons, is he
> Who stands confirm'd in full stupidity.
> The rest to some faint meaning make pretense,
> But Sh—— never deviates into sense.   (ll. 17-20)

Montague Summers has precisely stated the Mac Flecknoe problem: "Dryden, who very well knew what he was about, for purposes of his own cleverly dubbed Shadwell dull. And dull he has been dubbed ever since by those who have not read him."[12]

Earlier, Sir Walter Scott had distinguished between the satiric portrait and the man, but he qualified his praise of Shadwell in a way which suggests that *Mac Flecknoe* had indelibly dampened his enthusiasm: in writing "comedy he was much more success-

ful" than in writing non-dramatic poetry, "and, in that capacity,
I think Dryden does him a great injustice, . . . I think most of
Shadwell's comedies may be read with great pleasure. They do
not, indeed, exhibit any brilliancy of wit, or ingenuity of intrigue; but the characters are truly dramatic, original, and well
drawn, and the picture of manners which they exhibit gives us
a lively idea of those of the author's age."[13]

Shadwell's talent for holding a mirror up to his age was ap-
preciated even in his own day. A comedy by him meant a new,
incisive picture of modern life. George Etherege, writing from
his diplomatic post in Ratisbon in 1688, asked for a copy of
Shadwell's latest play, "that I may know what follies are in
fashion."[14] The play he received was *The Squire of Alsatia*
which, with its vivid pictures of London low life, has attracted
perhaps more critics than have his other plays. Macaulay read it
for details for his *History of England,* and Scott for some of his
novels.[15] The editors of a recent anthology which reprints *The
Squire* remind us that a "student must be grateful to Mr. Shadwell for painting scenes of Restoration life which would otherwise have escaped, and which are invaluable to the historian
and the philosopher."[16]

And, according to Albert S. Borgman, although Shadwell may
lack "the continued brilliancy" which distinguishes Etherege and
Congreve, "the reader cannot help feeling, if his interest lies in
social history, that Shadwell is one of the keys necessary to un-
lock the England of Charles II."[17] However valid the emphasis
may be, the persistent stress upon Shadwell's importance for
those concerned with social backgrounds takes away from his
greater and neglected importance as an artist who was deeply
concerned with the dramatic representation of the endless absurdities and the occasional triumphs of the human animal.
Shadwell is, above all, a satiric playwright; only incidentally is he
a "journalistic" recorder of contemporary detail.

To be sure, he was concerned with "realism," with what he
called "the common conversation of the World," but only as he
could utilize such realism in the effective creation of character
and plot and in the dramatic revelation of human folly and vice.
The locales of his plays are various—London houses and gardens,
apartments, taverns, streets, parks; the vacation resort of Epsom;
the fair at Bury; the forests and estates of Lancashire. Even more

various are his sharply delineated characters who represent many types and levels of society so that Shadwell's stage is a kind of seventeenth-century thoroughfare across which parade fools, villains, and wisemen from upper, middle, and lower classes—as well as libertines, fair ladies, effeminate coxcombs, braggart warriors, vulgar gamblers, dense squires, crude bumpkins, prostitutes, bawds, quacks, law students, lascivious clergymen, alcoholic Cavaliers, parsimonious veterans of Cromwell's armies, Spanish lovers, and North Country witches. The catalogue is long and full. And although Shadwell stresses distinctions between these types, ultimately he is more deeply concerned with similarities between them.

As his plays, particularly his comedies, show, social distinctions blur rather than reveal universal aspects of mankind. What binds together all members of his broad cross section of society is the "humor"—the psychological penchant which makes predictable their speech and action and which traps them in the irrevocable patterns of their eccentric personalities. The importance of his psychological concept of man cannot be overemphasized in an analysis of any one of his plays. As a Neoclassicist, he considered the transient details of contemporary life to be bright windows through which his audience could perceive and understand what was universally and permanently true of the human condition. The quintessence of his dramatic visions depends ultimately upon his skillful blending of details of modern life and certain undying characteristics of human nature. A consideration of his attitude toward folly and vice, of his concept of "humors" and of their place in drama, will make clear what these characteristics were.

After paying tribute to Jonson, *"The Mighty Prince of Poets, Learned B E N,"* in the Epilogue to *The Humorists,* Shadwell wrote:

> *A Humor is the Byas of the Mind,*
> *By which with violence 'tis one way inclin'd:*
> *It makes our Actions lean on one side still,*
> *And in all Changes that way bends the Will.*

This definition (which Shadwell supplemented in several of his prefaces and dedications) bears close study, for it incorporates all of the salient features of his method of characterization. The rhyming words *Mind-inclin'd* stress the psychological element in the delineation of comic folly, and the irrevocable penchant of this psychology (*lean on one side still*) is recognized as crucial to the dramatic action, to the changing circumstances of the play (*our Actions* and *all Changes*). *Changes* in environment reveal character because characters never change; thus *still* underlines the importance of consistency or "petrifaction" of character.

The last line is perhaps most significant for it hints at the philosophical implications of "humors" comedy. The *Byas* which dominates a man controls his will; it makes him emotionally and intellectually powerless over himself and against the forces of existence.[18] The phrase *with violence* is also significant for it seems to have been a specific answer to Dryden's charge that "forced" characters (extravagant eccentrics) merely shocked an audience, that they belonged in farces and not in comedies.[19] The definition indicates how much Shadwell wanted to intensify the specific folly, or "humor," in each character. Exaggeration was the primary and obvious technique in "humors" comedy.

"Humors" abounded in real life, according to Shadwell, but he distinguished between false and true ones by describing two kinds of human imperfection, the natural and the acquired. Natural imperfection—such as lunacy, blindness, or the physical deformities of "men born monstrous"—he disqualified as a proper source of comedy. It was rather *acquired* folly which was freighted with dramatic potential—all those imperfections which men ironically and unwittingly cultivate with painstaking assiduity. Man alone was responsible for his bad taste, his miserliness, his grossness, his villainy. From acquired imperfections no man was free, not even the wisest. It was, so to speak, a *condition* of fallen humanity that each man was imperfect in some way. The artist's task was to perceive and to re-create the imperfections. In the Dedication of *The Virtuoso* to the Duke of Newcastle, he underlined the moral, psychological, and social significance of the "humor" as an acquired characteristic:

I have endeavoured, in this Play, at Humour, Wit, and Satyr, which are the three things . . . which your Grace has often told me are the life of a Comedy. . . . [I do not] count those Humours which a great many do, that is to say, such as consist in using one or two By words; or in having a fantastick, extravagant Dress, as many pretended Humours have; nor in the affectation of some French words . . . . Nor is a downright silly folly a Humour, as some take it to be, for 'tis a meer natural Imperfection; and they might as well call it a humour of Blindness in a blind man, or Lameness in a lame one . . . . Natural imperfections are not fit Subjects for Comedy, since they are not to be laugh'd at, but pitied. But the Artificial folly of those, who are not Coxcombs by Nature, but with great Art and Industry make themselves so, is a proper object of Comedy . . . . Those slight circumstantial things mentioned before are not enough to make a good Comical Humour; which ought to be such an affectation, as misguides men in Knowledge, Art, or Science, or that causes defection in Manners, and Morality, or perverts their minds in the main Actions of their Lives.

Shadwell's comedy of "humors" is an exposition and a critique of man's deflection from wisdom and morality, of his incapacity to master his will and his existence and, above all, of the pride which blinds him to his imperfections.

Why a human being deliberately cultivated an imperfection and why he became the slave of his habit or ruling passion are questions which Shadwell never (or only obliquely) explored in his plays. A "humors" character is not created as a "case study" for complex psychological or psychiatric examination. A "humors" character simply exists. He is a puppet, the personification of his own comic flaw, a figure nearly "human," but ultimately only a mechanical, stubborn, and eternal fool hoping to shine brightly and wisely in a society crowded with fools. A "humors" character strains to prove himself capable of the ideal he claims to represent, but all his efforts backfire and prove instead his incapacity to be what he wants desperately to be. A "humors" character is the laughing stock of society, and yet, with comic irony, Shadwell shows us that those who laugh at him are usually equally stricken by their own ruling passions, are also objects of laughter.

Although we do not know the precise psychological origins of "humors," we learn that a source of folly is society—the world of people, things, and ideas. Society provides the settings and the paraphernalia in which the passion is born and in which it is cultivated. The dissembling gambler has his tavern room, his cards, and his dupe; the usurer has the coin of the realm and a bankrupt spendthrift; the would-be dramatist has the theater and words with which to compose incredibly poor plays for audiences without taste. To the symbolic settings of Shadwell's comedies—the parks, taverns, bachelor flats, and country estates —gravitate the wise and foolish characters, the fleecers and the fleeced, the moneylenders and the borrowers. The focal activities are social ones which draw out and distinguish the wiseman and the fool—commerce, religion, fashion, courtship, marriage, politics, sports, war, science, music, philosophy, poetry, and plays. Society caters to personality. It is an arena of action, a stage, and we witness in Shadwell's comedies the impact of "humor" against "humor" on it. And it must be remembered that no one, not even the wisest, wittiest hero and heroine, is utterly free from these ruling passions which compel specific patterns of action and reaction. Since they must function in society, they must deal with others on society's terms; they must, willingly or unwilling-ly, commit themselves to the stage of the world. But their potential for wisdom outweighs their potential for folly and villainy.

Shadwell's remarks on wise people in the Preface to *The Humorists* may well be applied to his idea of heroes and heroines in a comic universe:

'Tis true, excellent men may have errors, but they are not known by them, but by their excellencies: their prudence overcomes all gross follies, or conceals the less vanities, that are unavoidable Con-comitants of humane nature; or if some little errors do escape 'em, and are known, they are the least part of those men, and they are not distinguished in the world by them, but by their perfections; so that (if such blind-sides, or errors be represented) they do not reflect upon them, but upon such on whom these are predominant; and that receive such a Biass from 'em, that it turns 'em wholly from the wayes of Wisdom or Morality.

It is not difficult to distinguish between the hero and the fool of Shadwell's comic universe. Among other things, the hero main-tains a position of aloof observer in a world in which "humors" are constantly colliding. He does so, at least, in the early scenes; in time, he finds himself drawn into the arena of comic activity. Yet the essence of his "heroism" is that he never loses his sense of satiric amusement or profound loathing; and he never succumbs to the extreme absurdities of which most men are guilty.

II *"Humors" versus Wit*

Although Shadwell shared with Dryden and Etherege in the development of, among other things, the famous "gay couple" of Restoration comedy,[20] Shadwell specifically supported the aims and methods of the old Jonsonian approach against the modern witty approach to comedy, and it was against Dryden that Shadwell argued the case for Jonson. Dryden declared that Jonson had exhausted the limited vein of "humor" characterization, that his mode was too "old-fashioned" for modern tastes.[21] Dryden believed that modern playwrights had to perfect new modes of comic expression, and the great clue to these new modes was in the development of an urbane, brilliant, graceful, intelligent, and witty language. Such language called for witty characters, the sophisticated people of the play. He objected in great part to "humors" comedy because it relied chiefly upon low types, fools and villains who could not be expected to speak the language of wit. Bustle and crudity, not sophistication and wit, were the hallmarks of the old comedy. This distinction formed the crux of the early Dryden-Shadwell quarrels.

Shadwell's main objections to Dryden's arguments show that he believed that comedy should represent, above all, a variety of characters clashing in the absurd "wars" of "humors," conflicts which exposed most thoroughly the grotesqueness and the silliness of the human spirit. Such variety of characters could hardly be possible if the stage were given over primarily to fine ladies and gentlemen who were little more than mouthpieces for the playwright's clever style. He argued that wit comedy called for little in the way of diversified characterization and complex comic design. To Dryden's charge that the old comedy required little wit, Shadwell sharply retaliated as, for example, in the Preface to *The Sullen Lovers:*

Though I have known some of late so Insolent to say, that *Ben Johnson* wrote his best *Playes* without Wit; imagining, that all the Wit in *Playes* consisted in bringing two persons upon the Stage to break Jests, and to bob one another, which they call Repartie, not considering that there is more wit and invention requir'd in the finding out good Humor, and Matter proper for it, then in all their smart reparties. . . . [In recent plays] the two chief persons are most commonly a Swearing, Drinking, Whoring, Ruffian for a Lover, and an impudent ill-bred *tomrig* for a Mistress, and these are the fine People of the *Play*. . . .

Shadwell's comedies have their ruffian rakes and impudent ladies, their clever and urbane heroes and heroines; but these figures do not generally occupy a position in the foreground. The foreground is given over to the "humors" characters. In Shadwell's satire on science, *The Virtuoso*, for example, attention is drawn to the projector Sir Nicholas Gimcrack and to the florid orator Sir Formal Trifle and to the hypocritical masochist Snarl. Yet the play has two pairs of gay couples, four witty pranksters, who sneer at the fools in a language perhaps plainer than Dryden recommended, certainly in a style less brilliant than the style which a writer like Congreve provided for his witty characters.

Shadwell may have taken his stand against Dryden for the simple reason that he felt he was (or knew he was) deficient as a witty stylist. Yet he insisted that true comic wit depended upon the artist's ability to create character, upon "the finding out good Humor, and Matter proper for it." Perhaps he thought that Dryden wanted all characters to speak in the same way, and perhaps he was unable to recognize subtle stylistic differences between sophisticated characters. His obstinacy in this matter of style and characterization is in itself, however, illuminating if we wish to grasp what Shadwell believed to be the function of the gay couple in "humors" comedy. Shadwell's comic world, rich in variety of character, distinguishes between the wise and foolish person—but not so sharply or so conclusively as wit comedy does. In Thomas Fujimura's terms, the comedy of Etherege, Wycherley, and Congreve relies primarily upon his great contrasts between the hero (the true wit) and the fool (the would-be or the false wit).[22] But Shadwell did not draw so exact a line between hero and fool; not even the wisest persons were free from imperfections.

In Shadwell's universe, then, many ironic similarities between the wise and the foolish are drawn, many fine shades of difference between the philosophical rake and the rhapsodical coxcomb. A composite portrait of the Shadwellian comic hero points up some major differences between him and the typical "humors" characters.

III   *Heroes, Heroines, and the Comic Universe*

The hero is a libertine, espousing no traditional beliefs, despising commercialism of any kind, dubbing himself an "honest debauchee"—a man who would willingly deceive anyone who he feels ought to be deceived. He can be a cad and a criminal. He can blackmail a parent, abandon unwanted mistresses and illegitimate offspring, or woo his friend's wife or his fiancée's mother. More typically, he is a faithful friend and a generous one. He has little respect for the past—an attitude apparent in his mockery of old ideals or in his manner of wasting in a day a fortune which his father took a lifetime to amass.

Above all, he vociferously criticizes convention. Usually, his objects of scorn are middle-class merchants, fashionable fops, hypocritical clergymen, or foolish husbands. Often he indulges in harmless, low pranks or farcical plots to expose criminals and fools, becoming in effect the criminal or fool because only in those roles can he cope with the society he encounters, only in those roles can he play the game of life. Occasionally, he assumes the active part of devil's advocate, undercutting cherished illusions of human perfection and becoming a "scowrer" who occupies his nights by breaking good citizens' windows or seducing their wives. He wants to shatter the sense of orderliness and discipline which he believes that civilization falsely *imposed* upon the hearts and minds of man.

According to the hero, man is a reasoning animal born free to love indiscriminately, to scorn sacred things, to act wittily and wisely—that is, unconventionally. Unlike "humors" characters, he treasures his free will. Only natural passions can dictate his actions because he considers them the surest guides to action. He is the leader of an urbane, skeptical, essentially cheerful opposition to the false formalism of a universe overwhelmed by unintelligent or crafty pretenders and hypocrites. With something of the cavalier flippancy of the "Sons of Ben," the hero observes and accepts the great reality of life's transience; and he arranges his own brief life according to it.

The heroine matches perfectly the hero in most ways. She is a fine observer of pretense and folly and knows well the art of ridicule. Yet she is more serious about her life than the hero because, as a female who soberly prizes her virtue and reputation, she cannot enjoy his kind of liberty. Indeed, at the beginning of the comedy we find her usually caught in a parental trap in which she is the "slave" of a father, mother, or guardian whose tyranny is obnoxious to her independent spirit.[23] Her prime motive is to escape from this trap, but her only means is marriage. She sets her sights upon the hero, ironically the least likely of the males in her life who would willingly succumb to wedlock, the most hateful of the social conventions according to his naturalistic philosophy.

This problem brings to the fore all of the shrewd strategy she can manage. She must win the man who is singularly worthy of her. She astounds him from the start by being uniquely unlike all other women he has ever known. She is witty, insouciant, intelligent, beautiful, virtuous. She greets romantic love-making with sarcasm, calls his intentions dishonorable, and proves no easy conquest. Her rejections stimulate his aggressiveness, and he finally, and also ironically, surrenders to her. In part, these rejections are merely masks; in part, they are based upon strong feelings of doubt. She has few illusions about marriage or about him. Indeed, the possibility that he will reassume his anti-matrimonialism soon after their wedding is present even during the celebrations of engagements or marriages which conclude the comedies. Yet she is willing to pay the price for her mistake, if she must; her aim is to move out of the parental trap into a position as a wife where she can express some degree of freedom. Her movement must be cautious, sober.

The Shadwellian heroine thus complicates the comedy of love and romance with a seriousness of purpose deepened by her significant ideas of freedom and of the will to choose her "tyrant." What we witness in the course of the action is her triumph. What happens after the curtain falls is another question. A future as the wife of a reformed rake may well prove disastrous, but, since she knows that no guarantees can be made about the future, she is a daring, spunky young woman, willing to take a chance.

In the chapter entitled "Triumphant Women," three comedies are discussed in which the female most overtly dominates the course of the action; but triumphant women—heroines, servants, derelicts, and cuckolding wives—are typical of all of Shadwell's comedies. Occasionally, a knavish lady is punished by the laws of comic poetic justice; more often, she shares with the heroine the achievement of her goals. Prostitutes acquire aristocratic titles; lubricious ladies have fleeting affairs with the hero before he marries; pregnant mistresses find new fathers for their illegitimate offspring. The heroine and the prostitute both carry out their designs by using similar strategies—deception, tricks, masks, and plots which will win the object of their desires.

But the distinctions between them lie in the object of their desires and, often, in the reasons for their pursuit. Base women chase fools, and they win fools. And their victory is a punitive achievement, paradoxically a penalty rather than a prize. Bawds gain a reputation or a title, but they pay for it dearly by dooming themselves forever to foolish mates for whom they feel no passion. Marriage is solely a social or an economic necessity. They can never hope for a future better than the one they envision on their wedding day since the fools they wed, being "humors" characters, will never change. Nor will these women, being "humors" characters, ever want anything better than what they have known.

The hero is also curiously similar to, as well as significantly different from, the "humors" characters. He is the ladies' victim, the leading puppet in the heroine's plot. Submitting to naturalistic or deterministic impulses, he is not unlike the "humors" characters whose will is bound by a single point of view. The joys of wine or of the flesh drive the hero on; they mark the "bias of his mind." Yet, unlike the "humors" character, the hero is changeable. From his staunch anti-matrimonial position he moves into marriage, convinced, moreover, that the movement is wise. Like his bride, he understands the doubts that inform their future life. Is he dooming himself? Or is he becoming a husband, as recent criticism has suggested, with greater self-awareness, with an ironic recognition of the need of submitting to the social institution?[24] At least, we can say that he commits himself to the heroine with *awareness,* in contrast to his foolish counterparts who often do not even know whom they have married because the shrewd bawd disguised herself for the marriage ceremony. Fools are unwary. And, even though the rake may prove unfaithful and unworthy of the heroine's efforts to win him, she must prefer him still to the conventional, predictable, faithful coxcomb.

These observations on heroes and heroines, fools and villains, crucial motifs and recurrent plots may suggest that Shadwell's idea of comedy was *en soit* sharply limited in scope, that it offered few possibilities for variation of theme. Concerning the writing of "humors," Dryden said of Jonson that he "was the only man, of all ages and nations, who has performed it well, and that but in three or four of his comedies: the rest are but a *crambe bis cocta;* the same humours a little varied and written worse."[25] And we may suppose that Shadwell, who lacked the genius of his master, might (from Dryden's viewpoint) be more severely criticized for repetitive elements in his comedies as a group. In attacking Shadwell's heroes in *Mac Flecknoe*, Dryden spoke of them as "Whole Raymond families, and tribes of Bruce" (l. 93)—referring to two of Shadwell's heroes; and there is no doubt that the "humors" idea, the notion of the pursuing female, and the importance of the libertine rake suggest that all of Shadwell's comedies are grounded in an essentially similar attitude to human nature as the source of comic-satiric invention. Can we, however, agree with Dryden that Shadwell merely imitated himself with each new play?

The essence of Shadwell's plays, throughout his career, is to show us a world of fools moving in the dark, in pursuit of the wrong things or those that promise them only unhappiness. The idea of representing dramatically such a world seemed to Shadwell inexhaustible in its possibilities. All the comedies employ certain recurrent comic themes and devices—the conflict between appearance and reality, the eternal war between age and youth, the witty love chase, the collision of fool against fool, the dupe snared in the comic-villain's web, and many other such perennial patterns of comic action. Despite his occasional excesses, the rake tends to assume the role of *raisonneur*, although not without ironic overtones. Usually there are two pairs of lovers, both so worthy of the name of hero and heroine that they must be closely scrutinized to determine which pair is, in fact, hero and heroine. Even the names of characters are used again and again from play to play. Yet, once these and other recurrent elements are recognized as part of Shadwell's highly conscious art, it is easier to see that he was concerned with something else (something other than only traditional comic material).

In each play, Shadwell gives us a different, a special way of understanding his comic universe. In the early comedies, he studies the anatomy of that universe and offers ways of coming to grips with it. *The Sullen Lovers* proposes two views, the amused and the lacerated vision of human folly; *The Humorists* takes the idea of ruling passions as diseases, and it merges the disease-illness analogy with the curative function of comedy, in which wise men learn to abstain from dullness in order to retain their moral-psychological health. *The Miser* introduces us to London's underworld; it juxtaposes the criminal-"humor" to the idea of law and order and stresses the necessity of detachment from criminal folly. All three plays point to his later works in which criminal degeneration becomes a salient feature of Shadwell's universe.

Epsom-Wells, often considered a wit comedy, stresses human recklessness by locating its characters in a resort where they drink mineral water to sustain their promiscuity. *The Virtuoso* satirizes the follies of science. *A True Widow*, the most Jonsonian of the comedies, develops the idea of the art of crime with implications concerning the similarities between writing plays and double-dealing. The farcical *The Woman-Captain* shows how indistinct the line between heroism and folly is, while *The Lancashire Witches* introduces in Shadwell's comic mode antimasque elements, pungent political and religious satire, and a prototype of the reasonable country squire who espouses intellectual sanity as an antidote to religious, political, and amorous madness.

Beginning with *The Squire of Alsatia,* Shadwell highlights the question of education and the value of society for the reforming rake. *The Squire,* with its wide assortment of "humors," exhausts nearly all of his earlier ideas in its brilliant arrangement of comic types and intrigues. In *Bury-Fair,* Shadwell again alters the comic perspective by bringing together country man and city man in a clash of personalities and by introducing us to certain new types—the *précieuses ridicules*, the sentimental country girl, and a host of country fools. In *The Amorous Bigotte,* set in Madrid, Shadwell explores the universality of folly, in a land

Lovers as a psychological comedy, and indeed the saturnine chief source of dramatic conflict. The plot is unusually slight for a Restoration comedy. Emilia and Stanford, two confirmed misanthropes, are constantly hounded by a mob of fools. They soon discover in each other perfect mirrors of their own moody temperaments, form an alliance to fight the fools, and finally agree to marry. Together, as husband and wife, they plan to escape from London, the setting of the play, the symbolic center of impertinence and the heart of civilization which breeds, like a disease, the fashionable coxcombs of the world.

The Sullen Lovers is Shadwell's first comic examination of a strong misanthropic attitude, just as his adaptation of Shakespeare's *Timon* is his first and only examination of this attitude from a tragic point of view. The lovers' misanthropy, the growth of their affection and their decision to marry are reflected in the structural arrangement of the action of *The Sullen Lovers*. In Act I, the pair, independent of each other, rail against social impertinence. Stanford wants to escape to a deserted West Indian island; Emilia, reading her favorite book, Burton's *Anatomy of Melancholy*, contemplates retirement to a nunnery. Both cherish privacy. Both hate society. Yet neither wants to reform society, for they both see nearly all men as fools and fools cannot be reformed. As Carolina, Emilia's younger and wittier sister, succinctly observes of the sullen pair, "their very Principles are against all Society." And, indeed, they refuse to play the game of social intercourse, abhoring the truism that society is an arena for the impact of individual against individual.

In spite of their aversion (perhaps ironically because of it), they draw magnetically to them a variety of eccentrics. The egomaniac heroic dramatist, Sir Positive At-All, leads the assaults against Stanford; and Lady Vaine, the harlot posing as a "precise" aristocrat, leads the assaults against Emilia. The sullen pair first meet in Act II and their crucial alliance is formed. Acts III and IV examine closely the growth of their love. Although they occasionally suspect each other's "honest" misanthropy, both learn the value of dissembling as the only way of warding off fools. Two against the world, they are driven inevitably to marriage in Act V.

Yet there are pressures, aside from the impertinents, which drive them. Carolina and Lovel (Stanford's only friend) also wish to marry, but the sisters' father "has vow'd," according to Carolina, "never to Marry me till he has dispos'd of my Elder Sister." This gay couple then encourage the fools to plague relentlessly the sullen pair, and so they are the key agents in creating the Emilia-Stanford marriage. When the father tries to force Emilia to marry an avaricious impertinent from the country, she realizes that marriage to Stanford is her wisest hope.

The comedy ends with three nuptial celebrations, each of them establishing the degree to which it is possible for men and women to adjust to the absurdities of the social whirl. The misanthropes will run away from society; Lovel and Carolina, the real hero and heroine, will stay in London, but will remain emotionally and intellectually detached from social folly; the duped Sir Positive and his bride Lady Vaine will remain trapped forever in London folly and so sustain their symbolic roles as arch-victims and arch-purveyors of impertinence.

George Saintsbury remarked that this play "has the bustle and 'go' which distinguish our author at his best,"[3] yet Shadwell's contemporaries thought that the play lacked "go," that the recurrent exposition of "humors" tended to retard the forward movement of the action. Shadwell believed that an emphasis upon character demanded a simple intrigue, and he feared that too many surprising incidents, too complicated a plot, would destroy the desired illusion of consistent, petrified characterization. These ideas he suggested in the Preface in which he defended the simple plot. He was soon to recognize, however, the value of creating a more elaborate plot for an even greater variety of "humors," as all his other comedies show.

Yet in *The Sullen Lovers*, imitating Molière's manner in *Les Fâcheux*, Shadwell promenades the fools one after the other before his audience, varying the pattern of their folly by presenting them in pairs, in groups, in combinations. The fools iterate (albeit with increasing absurdity) their self-advertisements, their "set speeches," their verbal battles. The "bustle and go" occurs, in effect, on a psychological level. And dramatic complexity is achieved in the impact of "humor" upon "humor" and in the persistent question that the comedy raises: what point of view *can* one adopt toward a world composed primarily of self-centered fools? The question is, in part, an esthetic one; in part, a "philosophic" one. Shadwell offers three possible answers to it in the figures of the three marrying pairs—in the harsh disgust of the misfits; in the blind commitment to folly of Sir Positive and Lady Vaine; in the amused detachment of the gay Lovel and Carolina. Their detachment permits them to "live in the world," to observe it as an audience observes a play, to stand between the extremes of utter rejection of and utter participation in society. Shadwell recommends this amused view as the best view, although he does not ideate it. For Lovel and Carolina are not flawless; they share, though very slightly, the sins of their society. Like all the other characters (including the misfits), they *intrude* into the lives of others. As its subtitle, *The Impertinents,* suggests, *The Sullen Lovers* tells us that society makes every man, to some extent, an impertinent.

In the opening scene in Stanford's lodging, Shadwell expresses dramatically the philosophic bases upon which the action that follows may be evaluated.[4] Stanford and Lovel reveal their attitudes to society, defining by contrast and comparison, their comic penchants. Stanford's opening lament crystallizes the salient features of his personality and attitude: "In what Unlucky Minute was I born,/To be tormented thus where e're I go?" He hates the "Impertinent Age" and thinks man's best companions are bears and wolves. His tone of romantic-melodramatic self-pity and his non-conforming pride are sustained throughout the play and are duplicated in similar outbursts by Emilia. Stanford is an outsider, and life is, among other things, a prison and a hell where he is being martyred by society's demonic creatures. Or so his figurative language recurrently suggests. A modern Diogenes, he spends his hours combing London for an honest man, but he finds only irrelevant people either too frivolous or too hopelessly serious, men wiling away their hours at cards or in inanely abstract political debates. Stanford loves the theater, but finds only poor plays, inferior acting, and a noisy audience. The court boasts of its "gaudy nothings." Nights in London are worse than days, what with their midnight funerals, bellmen, and roguish streetsingers who do not let him sleep. Country life is no better, for there impertinence is crass.

Stanford's unqualified indictment of human unreasonableness, pretension, commercialism, dishonesty, and noisiness is grounded in an implicit belief that man is incapable of keeping ideals of good sense, plain dealing, and, above all, respect for other people's privacy. He has no doubt that such ideals can be sustained. He believes that he, uniquely, embodies them. Thus his pride makes him as impertinent as anyone else, and he emerges from the first as a perfect "humors" character because he insists upon the virtue of his own psychological penchant and because he derides all other penchants.

Lovel, who responds with amusement to Stanford, posits a second view of life. He agrees that the age is impertinent, that man is absurd, and that society seems to exist primarily as an arena for the display of pretense and dishonesty. But to seek friendship among animals is as absurd as anything else. Lovel prefers to picture the world as a stage or a circus with an assorted cast of buffoons created primarily for *his* entertainment. He laughs at the "Monkeys"; "The Variety of their folly alwayes/ Affords new matter" for amusement. He does not care that the impertinents are inefficient people; he finds them efficient comedians. No doubt, Stanford amuses him too, although he never says so. He admires Stanford's plain dealing, but advises him to modify his attitude. Stanford is making himself "Ripe for Bedlum."

To adopt a critical position which brings so much pain is, for hedonistic Lovel, to have no view at all. With the flippancy characteristic of the Restoration comic rake at odds with conventional morality, he calls the age "as pretty an Honest/Drinking Whoring Age as a Man wou'd wish to/Live in," and tells Stanford to take delight in a world which no truly wise man would ever trouble himself over. The neat opposition between the friends—between frenzied enthusiasm and a less stern, an easier view of life—provides us with a double perspective with which to view and to estimate the brace of fools who arrive at Stanford's lodging immediately after this initial colloquy.

We tend to lean toward Lovel's attitude (we are even more detached as an audience than he is), but we watch the parade of fools not without a sardonic awareness that Stanford's estimation has validity and a profundity which Lovel's lacks. Clearly men like Woodcock, Ninny, Huffe, and Sir Positive have fallen away from the ideal. In them, man's capacity for wisdom has given way to his capacity for stupidity. Through them, art is debased and commercialized, and love is merely a fashionable experience. Each has buried his innate talent for goodness and wisdom beneath a congeries of artifice and frivolity. From this point of view, Lovel's insouciance is disarming. There is something vacuous in his remark, " 'Thank Heaven I find nothing makes me weary of/My life . . . ,'" an element of complacency too tidy and simple to permit him to recognize the seriousness of human defects. His witty view, often idealized by Shadwell's contemporaries and exploited in the Restoration comic hero, suggests in great part the *moral* failure of a popular attitude of detachment. Although, then, we must laugh at Stanford, we must also consider with some sympathy his diatribes against sinning man.

Apart from these ironic qualifications of the two attitudes, Shadwell develops an esthetic opposition between them: two artistic modes of comic recognition. Both men are satirists. Their tone and attitude, the masks which each assumes, suggest the two principal kinds of satire admired by the seventeenth century —the Juvenalian and the Horatian modes. Stanford's rails in the tradition of Juvenal—reacting violently to modern decadence and opposing to it his own moral sense. Like Juvenal, Stanford cannot achieve detachment; human failure is too horrid to laugh at or to pity. Lovel's view is Horatian, for like the Augustan satirist, he is convinced that few men can achieve greatness, that folly is typically human, and that urbane disapproval is best because one cannot take seriously the constant comic spectacle.

The Stanford-Lovel opposition is thus distinguished by the conflicting tones and attitudes of Juvenal's "tragical" satire and Horace's "comical" satire.[5] Before the comedy ends, Lovel and Stanford retreat somewhat from their firm satiric positions, but neither actually converts to the other's point of view. Stanford learns, for example, that fools can be used for achieving personal ends, particularly for winning Emilia. His marriage to her is in itself a submission to the social pattern. And Lovel also surrenders to the binding conditions of wedlock which he thought to be the perfect example of folly. The two sisters thus emerge as worthy figures out of the pageant of fools. They draw the men to them and to the center of social relationships embodied in the marriage contract.

The fools serve then to excite two strong satiric attitudes toward society. They are reminders also of the danger of not taking a satiric-philosophic stance, for they lack a satiric-philosophic attitude. Immersed in folly, they try perpetually to hide their deficiencies as human beings beneath a veneer of language and action which emphasizes the discrepancy between what they are and what they profess. Ninny, the poetaster, writes for money, but he strenuously declares himself an idealistic artist. The more he insists that his feelings are deep and his life is heroic, the clearer it is that his feelings are shallow and his life is comic. His poems themselves reveal his essential incapacities; they deal with the antithetic emotions of loving (now the lover is hot, now cold; now in pain, now feeling pleasure) in conventional oppositions which show him trivial and "unstable." He evaluates his verses according to their market price, ten shillings a line. Similarly, the effeminate Woodcock, incapable of any profound human relationship, fawns upon others, tries to conceal his emotional deficiencies under a shower of sugared compliments, politesse, and kisses. The Country Gentleman who wants to marry Emilia speaks gnomic wisdom, but he is really a narrow person whose only wisdom is money. Lady Vaine, Lovel's former mistress, pregnant and unwed, convinces only the blind Sir Positive that she is a virtuous aristocrat. Yet of all the fools, she alone is conscious of the difference between her appearance and her real nature. The others have convinced themselves that they are the wonderful people they claim they are.

Sir Positive embodies on a grand scale the follies of the other "humors" characters. He uses language chiefly as an instrument of self-advertisement, as the means of creating illusions of himself for public consumption. Yet this most loquacious of his tribe lacks neither the intelligence nor the essential talent for being a worthy product of civilization. For one thing, he appreciates Ben Jonson, a sign, certainly, by which Shadwell wishes to indicate Sir Positive's artistic wisdom. But what talents he possessed, he has misdirected; he has become a purveyor of, for Shadwell, the greatest of dramatic absurdities: heroic tragedies. In many ways Sir Positive resembles Stanford, for he too insists upon his uniqueness and idealism. But Sir Positive relies upon the approval of others; and, whereas Stanford finally realizes that he is not unique and that Emilia duplicates his disposition perfectly, Sir Positive never abandons his egoistic position.

Indeed, his claims to greatness grow increasingly hysterical in each act, reaching a climax in Acts IV and V. His catalogues of achievement read like an index to human action, from the serious activity of architecture and war to the trivia of dancing and stool-ball. Above all, he sees himself as the living hero of heroic tragedy, an *"Unus in Omnibus* through Arts and Sciences," a Jack-of-all-Trades. The success of this "humors" character depends largely upon our awareness that he is incompetent in all areas of human endeavor, upon his hysterical accumulation of "talent," and upon his unconscious self-imprecations (". . . if I don't do all these [things], and fifty times more, I am the greatest Owle, Pimp, Monkey, . . . or what you will; spit upon me, kick me, cuff me, lugg me by the eares, pull me by the Nose, tread upon me, and despise me more than the World now values me"). In perhaps the finest satiric scene of the comedy in Act III, he challenges two clerks to a duel because they railed at his heroic play, *The Lady in the Lobster.* But Sir Positive is no fighter; he convinces the baffled clerks to sign a legal document attesting to his dramatic genius. From the Horatian view, Positive is an overwhelming fool; from the Juvenalian, his egomania points to something more serious, to that tyrannic madness which many seventeenth-century thinkers considered the most terrifying of dangers to the peace of mankind.

That Shadwell saw this egomania as just such a threat is suggested in the Preface where, decrying dogmatism in literary criticism, he remarked: "positive Men, that justifie all their faults, are Common Enemies, that no man ought to spare, prejudicial to all Societies they live in, destructive to all Communication, always endeavouring Magisterially to impose upon our Understandings, against the Freedome of Mankind: These ought no more to be suffer'd amongst us, then wild beasts: for no corrections that can be laid upon 'em are of power to reforme 'em." But this positive fool, by comic transmogrification, is made to undermine repeatedly his fantastic claims to superhumanity ("I tell you all Elements are alike to me, I could live in any one of 'em as well as the Earth") and destructiveness ("This single head of mine shall be the balance of Christendom: And by the strength of this I'le undermine all Commonwealths, destroy all Monarchies, and write Heroick Plays"). The satiric drop at the end of this outburst reminds us that, in the comic atmosphere of *The Sullen Lovers,* Sir Positive is harmless, no danger to the world.

His marriage to Lady Vaine illustrates in a different way the quasi-humorous, quasi-serious implications of his failure. Like the gay or the sullen couple, Positive and Vaine are cut from the same temperamental cloth. Both are pretenders, but whereas the knight has come to believe in his superhumanity, the harlot only *pretends* to play the part of a heroine to flatter his heroic delusions. His failure to understand her real moral and social position results in her entry, through their marriage, into the aristocracy. Positive's failure thus assumes larger meaning, and it suggests a theme recurrent in Shadwell's plays: the leveling of the social classes. The cause of leveling is usually, as in this case, traced to the conniving of the upstart and the naïveté of the aristocrat. Learning who his wife is, Positive's folly is finally underscored in his rationalization that "He's a wise man that marry's a harlot, he's on the surest side, who but an Ass would marry at uncertainty?" *Hubris* and the truth permit him no defeats.

Yet the grim "certainty" in his marriage is ironically contrasted to the "uncertainty" of the other two marriages. Both Carolina and Emilia know that marriage (even to men whom they love) does not insure happiness. Emilia agrees to Stanford's proviso in Act V that, if after marriage "either grows a Fopp, the other shall have liberty to part." And Carolina never loses her fear that her reformed, amused rake may someday find that she too is a "Monkey," an object of comic satire. In her verbal love-duels with Lovel, she conceives of herself as a bargaining agent in a commercial situation. She boasts in Act II of "all the treasures of her Youth and Virginity, which have been preserv'd with so much Care, and Heav'n knows, some trouble too . . . ," refusing to give over these treasures to Lovel who wishes to possess them without payment, that is, without marriage. Lovel, eschewing commercial imagery, attempts to elevate his sentiments by using heroic-romantic-religious images. Like so many witty Restoration heroines, however, Carolina sardonically rejects his "heroic" style. The romantic illusion which blinded Sir Positive cannot blind this practical girl. She is not displeased with Lovel's attentions, but she is as urbane, as Horatian, in her mode of regarding the world as he. Like all of Shadwell's comic heroines, she knows that she must cautiously choose her husband, that she has but one choice in the crucial change of roles from obedient daughter to obedient wife. Yet in a world of fools, Lovel is the finest offering, and she knows that the future promises nothing certain for anybody.[6]

She translates her skepticism into a dramatic image at the end of the comedy. As master of ceremonies she provides a wedding entertainment, but "in stead of a grand Dance according to the laudable Custome of Weddings, I have found out a little Comical Gentleman to entertain you with." A *"Boy in the habit of* Pugenello" then *"Dances a Jigg."* Significantly, Carolina rejects a conventional, joyous celebration which will conceal the darker aspects of the future. In the figure of Punch, a character out of the improvisatory *commedia dell'arte,* she stresses her witty-malicious attitude.[7] Pugenello, a grinning zany, is as laughable and witless as any one of the impertinents. Like Carolina and Lovel, he *improvises* from the material at hand, using his folly and that of others to create some kind of dramatic excitement. But his witlessness, also a subterfuge or a mask, is only half of his real nature. Beneath the mask he is cynical, cruel, and heartless in his mockery of human achievements. The "triumph" of the gay and sullen lovers remains, indeed, a triumph, but it is punctuated also by Pugenello's presence. Shrewdly, ironically, and above all impertinently, he reminds us that what we call good fortune may ultimately be bad.

II   The Humorists *and Diseases of Character*

Shadwell's tendency to repeat certain elements from one comedy to the next is evident in his second comedy. As in *The Sullen Lovers,* there is a band of impertinents, "useless" and idle persons who publicize their non-existent virtues and who function as the instruments that bring together the wiser lovers. But there are also marked differences between the plays which indicate Shadwell's desire to utilize more fully certain dramatic materials at his disposal. In *The Humorists* there are more "humors" characters, and they assist in creating the illusion of a very crowded world of fops and lewd women. With these additional characters, Shadwell complicates the symbolic-comic interrelationships of the play, particularly in the elaborate low plot, and he develops with greater intricacy the symbolic significance of the setting, the action, and the language. What characters do

and say matters more, from a metaphoric point of view, than in
The Sullen Lovers. And the study of human folly, based upon
the notion of the "humors" as diseases, is underscored in the
metaphoric patterns of the dialogue.

Most of the action occurs in the home of the Loveyouths. The
middle-aged Lady Loveyouth, believing that her husband Sir
Richard is dead, repudiates her vows to remain a widow and sets
her sights upon the hero Raymund. When she discovers that
Raymund is hotly in pursuit of her niece and ward Theodosia,
she establishes herself as a "blocking character," the obstacle between the lovers.[8] In the hope of marrying off Theodosia, she
invites to her house the comic suitors: the foppish artist Drybob
(a play perhaps on Dryden's name), the would-be gentleman
Briske, and the disease-ridden man-about-town Crazy. These
men repel Theodosia, whom Shadwell creates as something of
a cross between Emilia and Carolina. She loathes the impertinents and considers them serious threats to her freedom of
choice in marriage, but she answers their presence with a wryly
cynical view of them and of the absurd situation in which Lady
Loveyouth has placed her. Theodosia's major defense against
them is language. She keeps the suitors at arm's length by
sarcasm, puns, and *double entendres*.

Drybob, Briske, and Crazy are responsible for drawing to the
Loveyouth house the low female characters who pursue them:
Mrs. Errant, a seller of used clothing, toys, and prostitutes; Mrs.
Striker, the wife of a dying haberdasher, who chases Crazy; and
Mrs. Friske, a young spinster, debauched by Briske, who lusts
indiscriminately after both Briske and Crazy. There is also
Bridget, the Loveyouth's maid, who cleverly arranges false
rendezvous and is largely responsible for the various marriages in
the final act, including her own comic "mismatch" to Briske.
There is Sneake, the first of Shadwell's caricatures of clergymen
but a rather pallid caricature compared to the powerfully conceived attacks on Anglican and Catholic clergymen in the later
comedies.

And finally there is Sir Richard Loveyouth, who returns
incognito from European wars and who, disguising himself as a
servant to his wife, moves freely between the high and the low
plots. With Lady Loveyouth he binds together both plots, observing silently her scandalous behavior until Act V when he

unmasks and banishes her from the house which she and her guests have defiled with "foolishness and vanity." The resurrected knight calls for a wedding dance to conclude the play as a tribute to Theodosia and Raymund. With them alone does he share a principal position in the high plot when the comedy ends, and he blesses them:

> All happiness to both, and may you be,
> From discontents of Marriage ever free;
> May all your life be one continued peace,
> And may your Loves each day and hour encrease—

There is grim irony in the blessing, for in the ambiguous word *Loves* Sir Richard hints at the possibility that the pair may be as unfaithful to each other as his wife was to him. His joy for the pair is mingled with the bitter knowledge that wedlock can be "one continued war"—even though Theodosia and Raymund are the only bride and groom totally aware of whom they married. Drybob and Briske wedded the veiled Mrs. Striker and Bridget, respectively, thinking each to be Theodosia. There can be no blessing for these men who call their marriages "Death, Fire-brands, Devils, Damnation!"

But even happy Raymund sees his marriage as a surrender to "fate," a *dying*—not only in the sexual sense of this word but as a figurative execution in which Theodosia is hangman and he is the criminal whose crime is to feel a passion which can be satisfied only by allowing Theodosia to fasten the marriage noose around his neck. Raymund and nearly all the characters of the play thus "run to their deaths," propelled by the criminal yearning and by the diseases of their ruling passions. The metaphoric language constantly calls attention to this conception of man's "humors." The dance in Act V does not feature the figure of Pugenello; but Pugenello's spirit, more comic than malicious in *The Sullen Lovers,* informs and animates the world of *The Humorists,* where it is often as malicious as it is comic. Our "humors," Shadwell tells us, cripple our personalities, control our wills, make us "sick." Society caters to our sicknesses, indulges them, cures them temporarily, punishes our crimes, and sustains our weaknesses. The disease-death-pain idea is not perhaps an essentially comic idea, but Shadwell presents it to us through comic lenses to show us the fundamental grotesqueness of human character which makes men want to "destroy themselves."

Ideas of diseases and pain, crime and punishment, in a society catering to and profiting by the ruling passions are presented literally in Act I, which is devoted chiefly to an exposition of Crazy's character and his problems. Crazy is suffering the excruciating pains of venereal disease, the punishment for his "crime" of lust, his lustful "humor."[9] He wants to be relieved of the pain, but not of the "humor." When he is cured, he will begin again his frenetic-comic search for love. Crazy, a minor character, so dominates the stage in Act I that his diseased presence is remembered throughout the play, and his explicit punishment is meant to reflect the implicit diseases and punishments of the other "sick" characters. "Humor"-as-disease and society as the breeding ground and sustainer of disease are expressed in the structure of the act, in the visits of the five people who come to see Crazy.

Mrs. Errant appears first. She is the woman who profits from Crazy's lust by selling him the commodities of infection, her prostitutes. In a strikingly comic, symbolic action, she kneels beside him rubbing his shins to ease the pain which she has helped to inflict. Crazy's second visitor is Raymund. He sees at once the grotesque implications of Mrs. Errant's consolation, and he chides his friend, "Ah brave *Crazy!* do'st thou hold up thy humor still? Art thou still in love with all Women?" Raymund does not moralize; his argument is "Epicurean." The pursuit of pleasures which bring pain is madness, the ironic example of man hurting himself. Such crimes are self-penalizing, and to avoid them requires a regaining of one's will. But Raymund himself is not immune to his ruling passion and to the pain which it inflicts. He calls his love for Theodosia a disease and compares it to Crazy's lust, employing witty romantic images in a travesty of romantic love. Crazy's sordid "wounds of love" are more painfully *real* than any knight's conventional emotional sufferings for his damsel. Raymund's own love is psychologically debilitating. His will is controlled by his love-disease, but he accepts romantic suffering with a smile and understands his situation with ironic awareness. Crazy's pain is too intense for smiles, and he lacks the ironic awareness of a hero in love.

[48]

Pullin, a French quack and the third visitor, is a product of society who exists and thrives on Crazy's disease. Pullen is always ready to take over where the Mrs. Errants and the prostitutes have left off. Once a poor French immigrant, he subsisted first on diseases like consumption by promising quack-cures, but he soon found venereal disease a far more lucrative illness in a world ridden with fools like Crazy. "Good Mounseur *Pullin*," Crazy rails in a passage typical of the elaborate catalogues of medical terms which inform the style of Act I, "do not I remember when you first set up for the Cure of this Disease you pretend to, with only Two pound of Turpentine and a little China, a few Hermodactyles, a pound or two of *Sarsaparilla*, and *Guiacum;* Two Glyster-bags, and one Syringe . . . ?" Crazy's expert knowledge of the Art of Curing the Pox has its comic overtones. Raymund also rails at Pullin, expressing his grim view of marriage (the institution toward which his passion for Theodosia is driving him): "you have learn'd some little experience, by Marrying an unsound English Strumpet, that was Pepper'd by some of your Ambassadors Footmen; she, by the many Courses she has gone thorow, has taught you something."

After Pullin is ejected bodily, Striker and Friske, the last two visitors, appear. They come in pursuit of Crazy, but are unaware of his condition. Their quarrel over the right to possess him rises to a grimly ironic climax because we see them as two lustful ladies contending for the right to be infected. They punctuate the idea that our "humors" drive us blindly toward pain and punishment. Some additional illustrations suggest the extent to which this core idea is proliferated and modified in the following acts.

All of the female characters have the distinctive power of destroying men. Raymund recognizes this power in Theodosia, calling it conventionally a "killing" power; her "Charming Eyes" cause him endless pain; if she rejects him, he dies ("Kill not a young Gentleman at first dash"); if she doubts him, he is "injured." He offers her "my heart with my own hands," a figuratively self-destructive surgical operation. Lady Loveyouth and the wenches are "ravens" preying upon their carrion, the male. For Drybob, women are an enemy army; only courageous men "dare venture to come within Eye-shot." This fop brings Theodosia a small French dog as a gift, unwittingly translating himself into the dog by insisting that both are a "sacrifice" upon her altar of love. Drybob pursues the dog-man metaphor by hinting that Theodosia's bitch and his gift-dog be mated. When she sneeringly rejects the match, Drybob answers for his dog who is "extreamly afflicted for the indisposition of her body." Such parallels between men and beasts, in which Shadwell submerges the disease-death metaphor, are frequent. Theodosia claims a dragon-like ability to "breath infection" and Crazy, arrested by the law for beating Pullin, is described as the proverbial rat in a trap.

Words in themselves are conceived of as weapons which can inflict pain. Theodosia uses them against the suitors. According to Drybob satiric poetry can decapitate an enemy ("I'll be hang'd, if . . . I did not write his head off"). A duel between Drybob and Crazy turns into a verbal battle in which they threaten various torments, including the ripping out of intestines and the amputation of limbs. Language thus brings them to the border of pain and death, but their cowardice prevents them from making the pain literal. Drybob especially thinks in terms of pain and dying. To stop a man from being witty is "as great a pain to me as stoppage of Urine"; and, when the love chase grows too hectic for him, he wishes that he were castrated. When the disguised Sir Richard informs Lady Loveyouth of her husband's death, she hires him to replace an usher who "dy'd last week for love of my Shoomakers daughter"—whether as a result of a broken heart or of venereal disease, she does not say. And Mrs. Striker, bored after two years of marriage, impatiently waits for her husband to die of a lingering consumption. Theodosia sees her hated aunt as longing for a new husband more "than a Son and Heir of one and twenty does for the death of his Father."

In Act IV, the settings stress ideas of darkness, death, and confusion. In the Loveyouths' dark garden, the fools hurry about in search of Theodosia, controlled by Bridget's farcical plot to confuse them and to bring the hero and heroine together. Crazy literally hurls himself over a wall believing that Theodosia is on the other side. Again he receives only pain for his passions. Mistaken for robbers, Crazy and Drybob are tossed into the cellar of the house. Drybob thinks that he is dead and in hell, and Crazy (pleased to bait his "rival" for Theodosia's hand) terrifies him by playing the Devil and swearing to punish him for his sins. A sudden fire breaks out and ends the act. The Love-youth house is saved, but its mistress' hopes of winning Raymund are dashed. Aware that he wooed her only to be near her niece, she calls for everyone to search for the girl, a "criminal," and to bring her back "dead or alive." For the lovers, it is Lady Loveyouth who is a "desperate disease" that "must have a desperate Cure"; the cure is to disobey her. The lovers elope and Raymund successfully tricks Lady Loveyouth into making Theodosia the legal heir to the Loveyouth estate. He accomplishes this by disguising himself as a legal agent; and, when he is unmasked too late, the enraged Lady Loveyouth attempts to retaliate out of spite by marrying Crazy.

The ironic consequences of her marriage to a "Walking Hospital" in which she shall have to learn the art of "physics and surgery" are prevented by Sir Richard's public unmasking. His resurrection suggests the extent to which it is possible to include within the comic context the *real* death toward which the "humors" characters run. The characters see that Sir Richard is not really dead, as we see that they are not really dying. His repudiation of sin and folly, his blessing of the bride and groom, his setting of his house in order—these are dramatic expressions of a desire to preserve some few ideals in a sick and a witless society.

III   The Miser *in London*

Of the many Restoration adaptations of Molière, Shadwell's version of *L'Avare* has perhaps the distinction of being the most original.[10] Although the "Foundation," the basic plot of *The Miser*, is essentially Molière's, Shadwell increased the number of characters and included vividly farcical scenes of London's underworld because he thought that *L'Avare* had "too few Persons, and too little Action for an *English Theater*."[11] He changed Molière's fairy-tale ending into a more sardonic comment upon the devious ways by which young lovers must achieve their ends in a society motivated principally by greed.

In Molière's play, the miser Harpagon is half villain, half buffoon. His obsessive lust for gold makes him unable to recognize or to experience any "normal" human relationships, for he judges all relationships in terms of gold. He tyrannizes his children Cléante and Élise, whom he wants to force into a marriage with a rich old man, Anselme. Aided by shrewd matchmaker Frosine, he plans himself to wed young Mariane; and, since Cléante loves Mariane, Harpagon becomes his son's rival. Valère, Mariane's brother, also feels the miser's power. Too poor to "purchase" Élise as a wife, but anxious to be near her, he poses as a fawning servant in Harpagon's house.

The structure of *L'Avare* is built upon a series of scenes in which the miser and his greed come into sharp conflict with all the characters—his children, servants, business acquaintances. Harpagon is broadly satirized, but not without subtler implications showing us that his obsession seriously threatens human happiness. He is soon shaken from his "isolation" as cruel tyrant when Cléante and La Flèche, a servant, discover and remove his hidden casket of gold. The loss throws the miser into a hysteria which reaches its climax only after Cléante returns the gold in the last act. The problems of the four lovers are solved by Anselme. In a conventional recognition scene, he is re-united with his long-lost children, Mariane and Valère. Anselme embodies the ideal of the good and generous father, protector of kin, who will rejoin joyously his wife. These happy endings separate him and the lovers symbolically and literally from Harpagon whose happy ending shows him standing apart caressing his fond love, his money.

No doubt Shadwell was attracted to this play because Harpagon's central position and his mania make him something of a "humors" character. Shadwell's miser is Goldingham, a London usurer; he stands firmly in the center of a sick society; greed compels him to reach out in all directions, grasping at the lives of others and tainting them. Far more explicitly than Molière, Shadwell insists that Goldingham's disease is not confined only to his home, the center of greed. It grows and flourishes throughout London, among merchants, gamblers and bawds. Perhaps Shadwell's major alteration is the manner by which Goldingham's son Theodore tricks him into joining a fictitious conspiracy to overthrow Charles II. Profit is Goldingham's single purpose, the core of his reality. He is shown willing to destroy his king, not for political reasons, but for small profit; and so his greed reaches out even to the court and the throne, literally endangering the safety and sanctity of both. Such an explicit suggestion is absent in Molière's comedy.

Although Goldingham's greed isolates him from society—makes him anti-social—society is ironically the great source of his profit as well as his victim. His "humor" links him intimately to the outside world, to those who borrow from him and are ruined by him. Society is the market place for his greed. And between his debtors and his kin, he sees no distinctions. Indeed, unknown to him, Theodore is deeply in his debt; and, because Theodore is best acquainted with Goldingham's "humor," he realizes that he is in the best position to outwit him. Theodore traps him into the fictitious revolution against the crown, swears to denounce him and, unlike his French counterpart Cléante, the English son keeps the stolen gold for himself. In Shadwell, the son's triumph is also an act of larceny. Honest Theodore must soil his hands, stoop to the sinister requirements for an unconditional defeat of his father.

In Molière, Cléante and Valère share more or less equally the hero's role; in Shadwell, the part is decidedly Theodore's, for it is his criminal wit which finds the way to overcome the obstacles to his financial-amorous happiness. Shadwell omits entirely the figure of Anselme and the fairy-tale conclusion. Theodore is the agent of justice, but not without Shadwell's typically sardonic qualification of the nature of the triumph.

Molière uses but one set, Harpagon's home. Shadwell uses about six sets and divides the action between two worlds—the miser's loveless realm and the underworld. Contrasts between both worlds are frequent and usually ironic. The underworld is as ruthless as Goldingham in its strategy for fleecing dupes; but, because it frankly admits to its dishonesty and because it tempers dishonesty with rough good-naturedness and a code of underworld loyalty, it is significantly different from the morbid world of the miser. Goldingham's conception of his daughter Theodora as precious merchandise for sale to the highest bidder is not unlike the bawdy Mrs. Cheatly's conception of her daughter Lettice who is a confirmed prostitute. Neither parent-daughter relationship is "natural," and both are subject to satiric criticism. Goldingham's tyranny, however, is subsumed under the Juvenalian mode and Mrs. Cheatly's under the Horatian. The first makes us scorn the parent; the second makes us laugh at him.

The underworld is linked to the miser's world primarily through Theodore who moves freely between the two worlds. The underworld offers this lusty young man things unavailable at home—friendship, guidance, freedom, adventure, gaiety, a sense of honor (among thieves), and even love. It cannot provide him with virtuous ideals, but he finds virtue and an ideal in Isabella (Molière's Mariane) who exists in a world apart from the tavern and the miser's home. He knows well the dog-eat-dog atmosphere of London, but he turns his knowledge of crime into an instrument which overthrows the arch-criminal, his father.

There is poetic justice in Goldingham's overthrow. It results basically from his failure to guide his son, to provide him with the love and education which he seeks outside of the paternal circle. Goldingham's incapacity as a father destroys him. Yet long before the comedy begins, he has clearly forfeited his right and power as a father by setting himself up as the obstacle to his son's happiness. Theodore sees him as a dupe, a social enemy, his will controlled by a "humor" which has destroyed whatever natural paternal sensibility he might have had. This idea is stressed in Act V when Theodore and the other characters—except Goldingham—congregate over the ruins of his father's estate. Theodore impertinently borrows his "Fathers House for a Dance; for perhaps we shall never come in it again." The lines suggest the son's new-found independence: he will *borrow* without his father's consent; he will keep his father's gold without permission; he will start a new life as Isabella's faithful spouse.

In the underworld characters Shadwell comically caricatures aspects of aristocratic and middle-class life. The gamblers Rant and Hazard, Cheatly, her daughter Lettice, and the wench Joyce dominate the low plot (the fleecing of the miserly scrivener Squeeze and his dull-witted son Tim). The gamblers bring together the middle-class concern for making money and the Restoration rake's cynical attitude toward life. Like Goldingham, though on a more vulgar level, they study the weaknesses of potential dupes and prey upon these weaknesses. They are proud of their "honesty," knowing that most men mask their cruelty and immorality under a veneer of morality and foppish kindness. They see their livelihood as an explicit defiance of authority.

They love to rail at institutions, like marriage, which destroy man's liberty.

They lack the rake's sophistication and gentility, but they share his love of freedom which they cherish as much as Goldingham cherishes his money. In Act V, still free from marriage and from the law, they hurl good-natured criticism at their friend Theodore and at his marriage: "Now art thou, . . . for a year, condemn'd to eat and drink, go to Playes, to Church, and lie with thy own wife most unreasonable; But 'tis but having a little patience, and we shall have you amongst us again, as honest a sinner as the best of us"; "Farewel *Theodore,* thou art no more a man of this world . . . ." Theodore asks them to stop their "senseless Railing" which is "dull and common." He rejects the ironic possibility that all his efforts to win Isabella will become in time self-defeating, that the artificial institution which binds him to her will go against his liberty-loving grain. But like the heroes of the first two comedies, he knows that, although his future is unpredictable, his marriage is based on firmer foundations than the foolish marriages of Squeeze and Lettice, and Tim and Joyce. His bride's wit and virtue distinguish her clearly from the crudely immoral Lettice and Joyce.

The marriages of Squeeze and his son are marked by the general confusion of lust, money, and folly which permeates the comedy's atmosphere. Old Squeeze weds Theodore's cast-off prostitute solely to safeguard his reputation as a moral businessman; he metamorphoses through marriage his prostitute into his wife. Tim enjoys for a night the rowdy pleasures of good-fellowship, wine, and women, only to find himself married to Joyce on the morning after his first debauch. Joyce and Lettice quarrel humorously over their new familial relationship—Lettice is Joyce's new mother-in-law. We are reminded that, had Goldingham married Isabella, she would have been Theodore's stepmother, a chaotic denouement which only the hero's blackmailing prevented. Mrs. Cheatly also receives her share of love in the last act when she reveals her secret affair with Robin, one of Goldingham's servants; but, like the gamblers, she boldly rejects the artificial restrictions of wedlock.

Molière's Valère and Élise are duplicated in Shadwell's Bellamour and Theodora. In Shadwell's grim world, they owe their happy ending largely to Theodore's criminality, but their ending is also reminiscent of Molière's fairy-tale world. Anselme's revelations are a kind of *deus ex machina;* they transport the four lovers out of Harpagon's realm into a realm of abundant wealth, generosity, and love. The "implausible" reunion in Molière is re-created in part in the reunion of Bellamour and his sister Isabella in Act V.

Shadwell keeps these two apart for the first four acts, but, when they meet, new familial-financial problems are introduced. Bellamour (whose real name is Raines) explains that he has been away from his home in the North for five years, during which time his father died; and, because his father left no will, the younger brother has taken over the estate and "has inhumanly put my Mother and Sister out of the house." Bellamour has been searching for them "somewhere about *Coven garden.*" The younger brother's greed and unnatural treatment of Isabella and of his mother iterate the comedy's theme of the destructive power of avarice in family relationships. Bellamour assures us, before the play ends, that he will assume his rightful control of the estate and display a generosity which distinguishes him emphatically from Goldingham, Squeeze, and, more subtly, from the Rants and Hazards of London. He will give his sister five hundred pounds a year, according to his father's wishes—although he is not legally bound to do so. He is not restricted by law, but he uses his freedom (unlike the gamblers) to give rather than take. Natural attachments supersede legality and he would rather be "kind" than be merely rich.

Goldingham alone remains immune to any kind of attachment to people. Even in the single instance when he *seemed* to be forming an alliance with Isabella, he rejected the idea because of her poverty and because he could not marry "without a dowry." In many respects, he is cleverer than his farcical compeers, Squeeze and Tim; for he cannot be snared into a false marriage to the so-called Countess of Puddle-Dock (Bridget in disguise). His caution is an impasse to Mrs. Cheatly, who boasts of having the shrewdness as matchmaker of pairing off such unlikely figures as Queen Elizabeth and the Pope; the Puddle-Dock plot is, we assume, her single failure. But any admiration we may feel for the miser is soon forgotten when, his "humor" firmly gripping him to the last, he curses his children; runs "out in a rage"; and, brooding morbidly, shuts "himself in his Closset, and will not be spoke to." Harpagon keeps his "dear, dear moneybox," the fruitless object of an undying passion. The English miser's punishment is more distinctively moral and less ironic: the defeat of unrequited love. Like any beloved lady, the inanimate object of his ruling passion has been lost for good. Theodore wins his lover and his father's gold in a double triumph of passion *and* money.

My readings of the first three comedies are intended largely as an introduction to Shadwell's comic vision. Although he abandoned the simple structural design of the *Lovers* for more complicated patterns, he repeated many of the characteristics of these plays in his later comedies. Among others are the Juvenalian-Horatian opposition; the use of a symbolic center—an analogy or "humors" character; and the idea of hero as criminal. But most important of all is his method of creating the "humors" characters. From the moment they appear on stage, he makes them pronounce emphatically their follies. As the action progresses, he sustains our interest in them by increasingly intensifying the pitch of their madness and by showing us how unaffected they are by the changing circumstances of the dramatic life they live.

CHAPTER 3

A Few Wits and Plenty of Fops

S HADWELL'S next two comedies differ significantly from
each other in tone and meaning. Both *Epsom-Wells* and
The Virtuoso display a crew of eccentrics and two pairs of witty
lovers, but *Epsom-Wells* (modeled partly after Etherege's *She
Wou'd If She Cou'd*)[1] represents what may be considered Shadwell's single attempt to write a "comedy of wit"—which meant,
for him, to highlight clever characters and to keep low "humors"
characters in minor, secondary positions. In *The Virtuoso*, Shadwell returned to "humors" comedy. Nearly Swiftian in his bald
attacks on science and scientific projectors, he places Sir
Nicholas Gimcrack in the center of the action, much in the way
that Goldingham is placed in *The Miser*.

In the Prologue to *The Virtuoso*, produced in 1676 some four
years after *Epsom-Wells*, attention is called to the chief differences between the comedies:

> In the last Comedy some Wits were shown;
> In this are Fools that much infest the Town.
> Plenty of Fops, grievances of the Age,
> Whose nauseous Figures ne'r were on a Stage. . . .
> Such Fools as haunt and trouble Men of Wit,
> And spight of them will for their Pictures sit.

The focus is on fools in *The Virtuoso*. Witty men and women,
"haunted" and "troubled" by them but able easily to triumph
over them, serve as clever comments upon their misguided efforts to understand man and nature.

I *Epsom and the Holiday of Love*

In 1663, when Samuel Pepys visited Epsom Wells, a popular
middle-class watering place located about fourteen miles from
London, he observed the vacationing citizens strolling about

"without knowing almost what to do, but only in the morning to drink waters"; and his various remarks suggest generally the atmosphere of idleness and boredom which encourages the search for amusement among all of the characters of *Epsom-Wells*.[2] Indeed, the locale is of great significance in understanding this play. St. Évremond compared it to Jonson's *Bartholomew Fair*, because both plays, re-creating "various things that happen to several persons in publick places," achieve their unity principally in the setting.[3]

The public world of the Wells is a world closer to "nature" than London; it is a place to which visitors flock to enjoy for a brief while a release from the humdrum commitments of life, a place where they can bowl, drink, and love in imitation of the idle rich. As Lucia, one of the bright young lovers of the comedy, remarks in Act IV, the "freedom of *Epsom* allows almost nothing to be scandalous." *Freedom* is a key word, for the idea of freedom in love and in marriage binds together the high and the two low plots. The three plots, with their abundant contrasting characters and situations, accentuate and proliferate the meaning of freedom. Epsom is, symbolically, the site of freedom, where people unmask and where truths are revealed.

The first low plot tells of the cuckolding of two London merchants—Bisket, a haberdasher and milksop to his termagant wife Margaret, and Fribble, a domineering comfit-maker who has made his wife Dorothy his terrified slave. The merchants bring to Epsom their dreary personalities. They constantly drink and bowl, ignoring their wives who, in the free atmosphere of Epsom, manage to find amusement in short-lived affairs with Cuff and Kick, two "cheating, sharking, cowardly Bullies." Epsom attracts such rowdies as Cuff and Kick who come to steal wives and money from dull-witted shopkeepers. When the adulteries are revealed in Act V, the women are shamed into obedience and faithfulness, or so they swear. But Epsom has satisfied their secret lusts. And the husbands turn their marital misfortunes to profit. They plan to return to London, sue the bullies, and keep their wives who are "not one jot the worse." In this low plot, the portrait of impoverished marriages is emphasized. Epsom allows wives and husbands to perceive briefly the truth of their loveless and hypocritical liaisons. Busy London conceals this truth; in Epsom, masks are set aside. But in an ironic and comic way Epsom amusements and sudden revelations are transient, for the Fribbles and the Biskets leave the country setting acting as if nothing serious has happened.

The notion of temporary release from conventional attitudes about one's self and one's marriage is duplicated in the second low plot which tells of the clumsy misadventures of Clodpate, a Sussex Justice, come to Epsom to find a perfect wife. After futile attempts to win Lucia and Carolina, the clever girls who deride him, he turns to Mrs. Jilt, a London prostitute in search of a husband. She convinces him that she is a virtuous lady who shares not only his abhorrence of the city and its sins but his adoration of healthy country life. After wedding her, he learns the truth and breaks off the marriage by sending her away richer than she came. Clodpate quickly regains his lost freedom, returns to Sussex and to his good friends—his horses and his dog Tray. He learns little from his experience, like Fribble and Bisket. Yet his ending is relatively happier, for he will not be condemned to a life of perpetual cuckoldry with Mrs. Jilt. The "magic" of his brief romance with her ends when he leaves the amorous proving ground of the Wells.

The high plot treats of the ironic, witty consequences of the amorous pursuit of Lucia and Carolina by two rakes, Bevil and Raines. Unlike Fribble, Bisket, and Clodpate, these men appear never to have been committed to any practical or serious careers. Their lifetime has been a vacation from "business," and they bring to Epsom a lusty approach to living which other people never discover unless they come there. The rakes immediately attract the girls who prefer them to the dependable fools of the world, like Clodpate, but who express a thoroughly flippant view of courtship and marriage which (unlike the flippancy of Shadwell's Theodosia or Theodora) does *not* mask a sense of profounder feeling.

Of all the characters, the girls are most aware of the idea of freedom. They know that the vacationing atmosphere encourages transient romances, mere "summer" affairs, and so they remain essentially indifferent to their pursuers. Unlike the women in the earlier comedies, they do not get married by the last act. They hold off the ceremony, demanding a time of trial during which the rakes must prove their loyalty by good behavior. And, even though Bevil humorously insists that their marriages are

[60]

inevitable ("for one Fortnights conversing with us will lay such a scandal upon 'em, they'll be glad to repair to Marriage"), one suspects that the rakes will never reform and that there will be no weddings. In Lucia and Carolina is expressed a special kind of freedom—not a capricious but a precious love of liberty which can protect young women alone on a holiday. Epsom cannot rob them of their virtue, for they come armed with a wry and wisely selfish indifference to the reckless atmosphere.

Together with these four lovers, there is a satiric contrasting couple, Mr. and Mrs. Woodly, a young libertine husband and his lubricious wife. Both of them detest their married state, and both enjoy freedom's pleasures, Woodly as the rakes' companion and his wife as their adulterous lover. The Woodlys' unhappy marriage is brought clearly to the surface in Epsom; but, unlike the Fribbles and the Biskets, they refuse to fall back on hypocrisy and lies after the truth is made obvious. They announce their divorce in the final act and celebrate joyfully the freedom they regain in Epsom.

The atmosphere of scandal, sexual adventure, and freedom is suggested in the opening scene, a kind of prologue to the action. It is about nine o'clock in the morning; a handful of characters are grouped "*at the Wells*" sipping cupfuls of nature's restorative waters. The waters suggest the various kinds of real or ironic purgation which nature allows the characters. The waters are symbolic of forces which will come into play. While the citizens and Mrs. Woodly converse in the conventional and superficial tones of strangers at a resort, Cuff and Kick describe frankly the sort of freedom and amusement which Epsom promises them. They drink the health-giving liquid to purge them of the debilitating effects of the previous night's debauch. Nature restores their health, but it also sharpens their appetites for another day of cheating, drinking, and whoring. Observing women dancing in a field just beyond the wells, they offer some reasons for coming to Epsom:

Kick. Many a *London* Strumpet comes to Jump and wash down her unlawful Issue, to prevent shame; but more especially charges.

Cuff. Others come hither to procure Conception.

Kick. Ay Pox, that's not from the Waters, but something else that shall be nameless.

Cuff. I have a great mind to run roaring in amongst 'em all.

Huff. Thou hadst as good fling thy self among the Lyons in the Tower when they are fasting. They'll tear thee in pieces. . . .

This view of Epsom, in which vacationing women are turned into raging beasts, is established in contrast to the more genteel view of Epsom and of lust, expressed by Bevil and Raines, who are "torn to pieces" metaphorically by the beautiful, virtuous girls.

The bullies and rakes are aware of the animalism which informs their beings, but the rakes typically intellectualize their feelings and discuss them in a philosophy of human nature. Ordinary life—the life of Fribble, Bisket, and Clodpate—they decry as gross and meaningless. Against their pictures of the dull, practical man who is too cowardly to set free his passions and who has supplanted them with false illusions of worldly success, the rakes postulate a contrapuntal hedonism. Life is a vacation; the journey through life should not be made at "a damn'd dull Carriers pace." Clodpate is the main target of their satire, for he once felt an impulse to enjoy life; he went to London to try his freedom, but he was duped by city-wits and, defeated, returned to Sussex to spend his days railing with Juvenalian indignation at London's sins. Clodpate's moralism simply conceals his failure to be an immoralist. In contrast, the rakes want to light their candles at both ends, to live and die in a "heroic" blaze, rather than in a dull "snuff." The conventional *carpe diem* theme informs their images of rapid existence, but they apply the theme to modern life in a way which suggests the tempo of Epsom's freedom from drab realities.

Conventional also is the heroic-chivalric terminology which they apply to their existence. But Shadwell satirizes heroic ideals by thus juxtaposing them to the comic world, even as he turns heroic ideals to his advantage by showing us that the rakes *are*, in a sense, as heroic as it is possible to be in the modern world. Rebels in a conventionalized, irrelevant civilization, as brash as Dryden's noble savage Almanzor in the heroic play *The Conquest of Granada*, Bevil and Raines propitiate their hedonism in action as dangerous as a warrior's—in drinking bouts which "shorten" their lives and in hangovers which they liken to battle's honorable wounds.

Women also endanger their health; but, because they idealize beauty and love, they willingly sacrifice themselves, like Crazy in *The Humorists*. What they call "love" is, of course, lust—the temporary satisfaction of their animalism. Indeed, the temporariness of love is a perfect instance of their *carpe diem* philosophy, for it embodies their sense of transitory existence. Their lust is more "polished" than the lust of Cuff and Kick, but the rakes, unlike the bullies, are not indiscriminate lovers. As modern knights, they hate easy victories. The conquest of a scornful virgin heightens their sense of heroism. Their taste runs particularly toward married women, however, since the dangers of adultery intensify their pleasures. They have come to Epsom to woo Mrs. Woodly. Bevil cuckolds and Raines plans to cuckold Woodly, thus satisfying not only their lust but proving also their libertine principle that wedlock is a meaningless legal-ecclesiastical bondage which cannot restrain true freedom and passion.

In a second recurrent image, closely related to the images of heroic life, the wits express further the conditions of their hedonism and thus point to the meaning of *Epsom-Wells*. Hedonism is health, as is freedom; any serious commitments are forms of diseases. Their figures of speech recall, in part, the disease-death imagery of *The Humorists*, but these figures are conditioned as much by the Epsom setting as by the rakes' awareness that any form of commitment means the death of their freedom and, indeed, of their rakish personalities. The opposition between the diseased man and the healthy man is stressed in their idea of the "stock" of passion, an abundant stock which they liberally bestow on any woman willing to take it. They are merchants of nature, for their passion flows as freely from them as the waters from Epsom's earth. In contrast, husbands limit their health by wasting their love on only one woman, and indiscriminate bullies "run to their deaths" by destroying their health, through infection, then by curing themselves with pills and mineral water, simply to be "at it again" in a senseless round.

Equating their mental and physical health with material treasures, which they liberally bestow upon others, the wits consider themselves truly generous. In Act I, they advise Woodly to discontinue his association with the unhealthy fools of Epsom for, according to Raines, "conversation is to the mind, as the air we live in is to the body; in the good we by degrees suck in health, and in the ill Diseases. Wit is improv'd in good Company; but there is a Contagion in Folly, that insensibly insinuates into one that often converses with Fools, let his constitution of mind be never so good." Bevil disagrees. Association with "a Clownish-Country Fool" like Clodpate is harmless, for "The Murrain among Cattle is not infectious" to "an honest debauchee."

Although Bevil accurately estimates a rake's impregnability with regard to obvious folly, he is wrong in believing that a rake is wholly impregnable. On guard against obvious folly (the idea, for example, of Bevil's or Raines's taking Mrs. Jilt as a wife is unthinkable), they fall victims to Lucia and Carolina; and they move toward the greatest folly of all, marriage. The initial encounter of the two gay couples, in which they literally save the girls from the assaults of the bullies and play the parts of Epsom knights-errant, marks the beginning of the end of their impervious positions. They are shocked to find that the girls' protestations of honor are real, that they are "honest" virgins. The girls are under no pressure to marry; no father threatens them with forced marriage and no impertinents harass them.

The girls decide to reform the wits largely to amuse themselves. Lucia is more aggressive than Carolina, instructing them in the mysteries of virtuous freedom where self-control is the guiding tenet of action. To win their hands, the men must, she warns in the concluding couplet of Act II: *"Think not what's pleasant, but what's just and fit,/And let discretion bridle in your wit."* The girls do not want to quench the flare for living which distinguishes the men. They want to show that they are entitled to more than the usual hollow love vows designed to win their maidenheads. Nor do they want to lose their maidenheads and then be rejected as cast-off mistresses. Carolina counters their hedonism with surprising flippancy; she calls wedlock enslavement, and the liberty which she loves is "Not your lewd liberty" in which "you squander [your stock] . . . away upon every one you see." The rakes' attitudes are sophomoric and unworthy of these gallant girls.

By Act IV, the rakes begin to retreat from their positions, bow-

ing before rare virtue, wit, and beauty and comically adapting
their libertinism to the new situation:

> *Bevil.* Well, I love *Carolina* beyond all sense of modesty, so much,
> that I am resolv'd if she will, to turn recreant and marry her. . . .
> *Raines.* To forbear pleasing our selves to day, for fear of being
> troubled to morrow, were to adjourn life and never to live.
> *Bevil.* I am sure of the present pleasure, and but venture the
> future pain.[4]

They thus bring their *carpe diem* logic into the service of marriage. Yet it is clear that their talent for sophistry can easily turn
the same argument to the service of unfaithfulness *after* marriage. In Act V, they renounce "dear Friends, the World, the
Flesh, and the Devil," abjuring "Wine for ever, and drink[ing]
nothing but Almond-Milk" if the girls agree to marry. But immediately afterward, Raines goes off to keep a rendezvous with
Mrs. Woodly. He knows that he is too weak (or too much a
creature of nature) to resist temptation. The promises which he
and Bevil make seem as vacuous as those which young Woodly
made when he married.

The Woodly marriage serves as a persistent reminder of what
can happen when a lusty youth fetters himself to an aggressive
woman. The Woodlys' life at Epsom is characterized by a series
of false starts, by lies, by hypocrisy, and by the chaotic patterns
of farce which result from Woodly's hopeless pursuit of his
Cousin Carolina and from Mrs. Woodly's pursuit first of Bevil
and then (after the affair) of Raines. Epsom exposes their
adulterous adventures, and it leads them to a permanent holiday
from each other. They invert the wedding ceremony in the final
act, spoofing the many proviso scenes of Restoration comedy as
they "unbind" themselves from each other. The agreement to
divorce, according to Mrs. Woodly, is "the first time we e'er
agreed since our Wedding."

Their comic use of legal jargon mocks marriage and suggests
implicitly the real reason for their separation: they want freely
to indulge their sexual drives. Taking a parting kiss from his "old
acquaintance," Woodly celebrates his true freedom ("How easie
and how light I walk without this Yoak! methinks 'tis air I

tread"); and, after calling for a dance which ends this play without a wedding, he points up its "moral":

> Marriage that does the hearts and wills unite,
> Is the best state of pleasure and delight:
> But—
> When Man and Wife no more each other please
> They may at least like us each other ease.

The Woodlys' candid admission of incompatibility is contrasted to the hypocritical Fribble-Bisket resolutions. The Woodlys are too alike to be compatible; the merchants and their wives are unlike enough to create a relationship which ironically makes them compatible as a master and his slave are compatible.

More than Woodly and the two London merchants, Clodpate is drawn as an ironic contrast to Bevil and Raines, particularly as his character develops themes of freedom, love, and marriage. He is a full-blown "humors" character, one of Shadwell's most popular creations; he is a man whose libertine penchant was thwarted in London where he received beatings and gonorrhea, but he found a haven in Sussex as Justice of the Peace in service to the King and he transposed his defeat (and his "humor") into something else. He became a zealous satirist, masking his lustful desires in tirades against modern Sodom. He regards puritanically the Great Fire of 1666 as a divine punishment against London and annually celebrates the event. He hates pride, popery, folly, lust, and bestial joys—always, however, reminding us that he has rationalized himself into a moral man. Ironically, Bevil and Raines agree with him; but they are amused by sin and are successful rakes. They recognize as amoral what Clodpate calls "immoral"; to them, "sin" is an essential and necessary aspect of man's state.

Clodpate uses his hatred of London as a way of "testing" potential brides. If a woman detests London as much as he, then he assumes that he and she are perfectly compatible. This "infallible" test backfires with the usual perceptive irony we find in Shadwell's treatment of "humors" psychology. Mrs. Jilt masks consciously her love of London but Clodpate does so unconsciously. With poetic justice, he takes her at her word and proves himself the eternal dupe, cheated in Epsom as he was in London. Places are as "sinful" as their inhabitants. In Act III in a key scene in which Clodpate entertains Jilt with a fiddler who sings the praises of country life and cries down city sins, Clodpate proves irrevocably his failure to distinguish between pretense and reality, between art and human nature. The fiddler tells of *"The Clamours of War,/The glittering Court, the fraudulent Gown,/The Suburb debauches, . . ./And the noise of the men they call witty."*

Clodpate, who pities the fiddler, offers to save him by bringing him to healthy Sussex, but the singer recoils: "I was born and bred in *London,* and would not live out on't for five hundred pound a year." There is a difference between the singer and the song, the illusion the artist creates and the artist himself. But Clodpate, outraged by this "deception," turns to Jilt who, with greater artistry than the fiddler, blinds the bumpkin into believing that her words truly reflect her inner feelings. In a sense, Clodpate's righteous indignation, his Juvenalian vision, is not utterly worthless. He strikes the single seriously jarring note in Epsom's frivolous world where, except in Lucia and Carolina, the moral sense is completely absent. But, unlike Stanford in *The Sullen Lovers,* with whom Clodpate may be in part compared, his awareness of man's fallen state is undercut by a complete failure to see that he admires what he claims to hate.

II *Virtuoso, the Disoriented Man*

The Virtuoso blends together strong "wit" comedy (the romantic adventures of Clarinda, Miranda, Bruce, and Longvil) with a strong satire on man's futile efforts to understand the mysteries of nature. But the satiric element is stressed, and the romantic or witty elements serve as sardonic and even sometimes sentimental comments on the satire. This play is about the ways that people pursue things, knowledge, and love, and about the penchants that compel them to do so. Although it shows us varieties of approaches to living, these are subsumed under two major headings: the foolish and the witty-romantic.

These approaches are suggested in the opening scene in Bruce's apartment, the morning after he and Longvil have spent a night in the usual rakish manner. Bruce, more intellectual than

Longvil, reads aloud a Latin passage from Lucretius' *De Rerum Natura*. Lucretius is, to them, something of a saint, the great Epicurean, the singular man who best understood reality—the mystery of being human. They compare this philosopher important in the history of Restoration libertinism to the bevy of modern fools who pursue fruitlessly the study of science and who never understand the nature of things.[5] The passage from Lucretius underscores, in interesting ways, the Classical position which the wits adopt: "it is essential to the very nature of the deity [Nature] that it should enjoy immortal existence in utter tranquillity, aloof and detached from our affairs. It is free from all pain and peril, strong in its resources, exempt from any need of us, indifferent to merits and immune from anger."

The view conflicts with the Cartesian belief that nature's mysteries may ultimately be revealed, or so the wits implicitly believe; between man and nature stands an insurmountable and (in the nature of things) necessary barrier. The wits translate nature's position vis-à-vis man into their position vis-à-vis society; that is, they imitate nature in a social context, posing as aloof observers of a comic world. Most men cannot thus imitate nature; they search for her mysteries, are bound in pain and peril by their own and other people's follies; their resources are weak; they are susceptible to passions which blind them to their own folly.

Lucretius embodies also a Classical ideal of wisdom sensibly expressed, for he is the "profound Oracle" who "reconcil'st Philosophy with Verse, and dost, almost alone, demonstrate that Poetry and Good Sence may go together." Not so most men, mere pretenders to wit and knowledge, who have neither truths to express nor the proper mode of expression. Or, if they have some truths, they express them clumsily; if adept at expression, they have nothing wise to say. Bruce and Longvil also "pretend" to truths, social and psychological truths about modern life; and, like the satirists that they are, they err perhaps on the side of a comic exaggeration of human failings. Yet clearly they too are objects of satire, guided by naturalistic passions and barely aware of the horrid humanity which they will soon encounter in the Virtuoso, Sir Nicholas Gimcrack.

The rakes examine the dangers of libertinism, but distinguish themselves from most "hot-headed" youths who return from

Paris "with a little smattering of that Mighty, Universal Language, without being ever able to write true *English*"; and true English they equate, not unpatriotically, with Lucretian good sense. They mock sixteen-year-old "Men of the Town," "the only Animals that live without thinking," who speak non-sense and vulgarity: "a form, a fashion of Wit, a Rotine of speaking, which they get by imitation; and generally they imitate the extravagancies of witty Men drunk." Yet Longvil and Bruce accept these "sad Truths" and consider them inherent in "the Beastly, Restive World." "Thank Heav'n," Longvil remarks, "I am not such a publick spirited fop, to lose one moment of my private pleasure for all that can happen without me," and his friend assents to this Lucretian wisdom.

But the wits soon give up their roles as fleering observers. By falling in love with Clarinda and Miranda (whose names hint at a "clarity of vision," intuitively Lucretian in its understanding of nature and society), they share in human folly. Their pursuit brings them, indeed, face to face with Sir Nicholas, the girls' guardian and uncle. In order to gain entry into his house, they pose as dabblers in science and soon discover in the Virtuoso the ultimate degeneration of the scientific spirit. Sir Nicholas has reached the very nadir of misunderstanding nature; he wastes his time and money on inane scientific projects and is compelled to know what Lucretius said man could never know.

In creating Sir Nicholas, Shadwell joined such contemporaries as Andrew Marvell and Samuel Butler in satirizing certain activities of the Royal Society.[6] Research has shown that many of the ridiculous experiments described in *The Virtuoso* were drawn from actual experiments recorded in such works as the Society's *Philosophical Transactions* and, in particular, Robert Hooke's *Micrographia*.[7] This blending of fact and dramatic characterization stresses Shadwell's serious, direct indictment of his age's comic-horrendous manner of tampering with nature's secrets. But the experiments are not the heart of his age's failure, from a Lucretian point of view: the failure lies in Sir Nicholas' character, in his way of making science a mere hobbyhorse and of deflecting attention from far more serious considerations proper to the intelligent animal, man. Sir Nicholas boasts unwittingly that his art is purely speculative. He claims to abhor the thought of a practical (or meaningful) application of his studies: "I seldom bring any thing to use, 'tis not my way, Knowledge is my ultimate end." He constantly incriminates himself by insisting that his knowledge is *useless;* and the experiments are all symptomatic, or symbolic, of his great folly.

The wits first meet him in Act II in his laboratory where he is taking a swimming lesson from a frog. He denigrates himself and his species by depending upon a lower one to teach him the Art of Swimming. His blood transfusions offer another of the countless examples of his failure to understand the human position. He prides himself on having metamorphosed a Spaniel into a Bull-Dog and on having transfused sheeps' blood into a madman which turned the madman "sheepish"—indications of his ghoulish proclivities. Indeed, the sheepman "bleated perpetually, and chew'd the Cud: he had Wool growing on him in great quantities, and a *Northamptonshire* Sheeps Tail did soon emerge or arise from his Anus or humane Fundament." When his Uncle Snarl (a character like Clodpate, and one of Shadwell's severest critics of modern society) accuses Gimcrack of lying, the nephew offers proof of a letter from the sheepman who is sending him his wool. The Virtuoso plans to create a flock of sheepmen and make "all my Clothes of 'em." Snarl reminds him that his transfusions have killed at least four or five men, a fact which Gimcrack does not deny, so that the seemingly innocuous curiosity becomes a dangerously homicidal incapacity to recognize the dignity of the human beast.

Many of the projects *are* innocuous; the Virtuoso is more to be ridiculed than feared. He bottles and labels air from various English resorts and treats his guests to breathing it. He discovers light in decayed matter. He has a Stentrophonical Tube (a loudspeaker) that carries his voice for miles, and a machine through which he observes the moon and reports on the activities of its tyrannic monarch. His mind on the moon, he misses what is going on on earth. His thoughts on the life of ants and tarantulas, he severs himself from the life around him. He went to Italy and spent his hours there collecting specimens for study, but he failed to study men and manners, the first concerns of the true philosopher.

Like Goldingham in *The Miser*, he pays the penalty for his "humor." In the last act, he finds his world crumbling about him, the world he refused to pay attention to. His wife (who has been cuckolding him with a kept-lover Hazard and with Bruce and Longvil) accuses him of marital disobedience by revealing his love letters to his mistress, Flirt. Because of debts incurred in the extravagant experiments, his estates are seized. His Uncle Snarl marries Figgup, his whore, and disinherits Sir Nicholas. And his last financial hopes, his wards, transfer their guardianship to Bruce and Longvil so that he loses their income by which he expected to pay his debts. His wife deserts him, and even his mistress does so because her business is to love for money and he is penniless.

Completely alone, it appears for a moment that these catastrophic reversals have taught him a lesson and that he will be able to crush the scientific "humor" that controls him. "Well, now 'tis time to study for use," he begins his last speech; and yet, before he concludes it, he makes clear that he can never change, can never understand the nature of the world around him: "I will presently find out the Philosophers Stone; I had like to have gotten it last year, but that I wanted *May-Dew,* it being a dry season." His "humor" is incurable.

In many ways, the Virtuoso is like the young would-be wits whom Bruce and Longvil describe in Act I, for he shares their prodigality and absurdity, but he is an older man and his folly is "great" in a serious way. He has rank, intelligence, energy, a potential for being wise; and thus he shares with men like Lucretius certain other characteristics—a curiosity about the nature of things. But his method makes him a caricature of the philosopher. If we measure the fall of the tragic hero by an overreaching pride, we must measure the fall of this comic character in the same way. His desire to *know* is inordinate; his desire to know about things that do not matter is inordinate. His indifference to the practical value of his search for knowledge is not the indifference of "nature," of the rakes, or of Lucretius; his is an indifference to reality.

Like Gimcrack, the other "humors" pursue knowledge or express it with equal indifference but with a similarly warped view of life. In short, they have no knowledge. Sir Formal Trifle, Sir Samuel Hearty, and Snarl serve, each in a different way, to illustrate the central thesis of the play: the degradation of the Lucretian-Epicurean ideal of wit and wisdom. Trifle, the most striking of the three, has been described as "an ever-memorable figure of high fun," whose imposing "largeness and solidity" are so sharply etched that they "enlist our sympathy and . . . make us forget the great native foolishness which motivates the character."[8]

Trifle is a man without knowledge, or, more accurately, a man who exploits in florid Ciceronianisms the very minute knowledge he has. He can turn a brief greeting into a lengthy oration, unable to distinguish between trivia and what might perhaps require florid exposition. His name indicates exactly his "humor"; and, unlike Lucretius, he cannot express wisdom in a wisely controlled style. He flatters his friend Gimcrack and introduces him to the rakes, thus unwisely bringing into the scene his rival for Clarinda. Trifle is the obstacle to the wits' successful courtship because he will not leave them alone with the girls.

In a scene which Dryden made famous at the end of *Mac Flecknoe,* Shadwell creates a vivid comic action between the man of words and the four gay people.[9] The lovers bait Trifle by flattery into expiating on any topic—they so admire (they insist) his style. When Clarinda suggests "a Mouse inclosed in a Trap," Trifle, in the longest speech in Shadwell's plays, tells ornately the trite account of "the uncautious Animal" enticed "to its sudden ruine" by the "specious Bait of *Cheshire*-Cheese." He is so lost in words that he does not realize that *he* is the mouse, enticed by his rage for eloquence, and that he is standing on a trapdoor which the gay foursome suddenly release. Like the devil in a morality play, Trifle sinks to his doom; and this literal fall in Act III foreshadows his second fall in Act V when he is tricked into marriage by Betty, a common, uneloquent woman. Like the Virtuoso, Trifle is betrayed by a "humor" that blinds him to what he is saying and doing.

Sir Samuel is a would-be gallant who prides himself on a talent for intrigues and masquerading, but who cannot mask his crudity and tactless love-making. A pursuer of the girls, he is outwitted by the real gallants; as a blunt and plain-speaking knight, he stands in absolute contrast to Sir Formal. Like Sir Formal, he has nothing important to say; and, like Sir Nicholas, his adventures are trivial. His presence in the play reminds us that plain-speaking hides the fact of an empty brain no better than circumlocution or scientific jargon. Sir Samuel is, literally, an "outsider" in the matter of courtship. The four lovers speak in his presence a metaphoric language of love which he cannot understand. Metaphors protect them from his impertinent intrusions.

Snarl is also crass, but his crassness is compounded by a virulently Juvenalian view of life. In his venomous criticism of modern decadence, he shows, in part, the awareness of the rakes. He has what the other "humors" lack, a socio-historical view of things; and he judges his own "moral" last age by the present immoral age. Like all of Shadwell's satiric ranters, Snarl, in his frenzy and indignation, is an invaluable commentator; but he lacks the detachment of the witty, Horatian attitude and, hypocritically, he is himself as guilty of dissipation as the age which he castigates. The rakes argue with him that the last age and the modern age were both immoral, but that formerly morality was used to conceal sin. Modern profligates possess at least the virtue of sinning openly and unhypocritically, of being temperamentally and intellectually blasé and indifferent to those noble, but unlikely, ideals expressed by Snarl. In time, the wits' accurate judgment concerning hypocrisy and morality is proved when Snarl's romance with Figgup is revealed. She satisfies Snarl's masochistic sexual delights by flaggelation, but even she, a jaded lady, expresses her distaste for such perverted loving.

Loving, then, like knowledge, undergoes satiric scrutiny in the comedy, and both are distinguished conventionally as emotional and intellectual forces. Yet loving, like knowing, can be variously understood and differently expressed. In the rakes, loving is a way of knowing and of achieving ironic recognitions of nature's mysteries. Although they stand by their Lucretian intellectual-social ideals, love shatters them emotionally and traps them into a position which jeopardizes their precious freedom as bachelors. Love drives them as potently as curiosity drives Sir Nicholas. Love creates comic reversals, the sharpest of which occurs when the young men "switch" the object of the love. At first, Longvil woos the disdainful Miranda and Bruce the disdainful Clarinda. But the girls' disdain is *real*—not simply a pretense to madden the lovers. Miranda loves Bruce; Clarinda, Longvil. Their disdain, in the first four acts, is intended to encourage their pursuers to switch from one to the other. In Act V, the men realize that they have been lavishing themselves on the wrong women; they shift their affections, rationalize the change, and then begin with renewed passion to woo the *other* girl. Their initial "blind" pursuit turns into a more meaningful one; but the turnabout shows also an incapacity to see clearly what it is they love.

Unlike the girls in *Epsom-Wells*, Clarinda and Miranda have specific reasons for attracting the men. They are literally the prisoners of a cruel and jealous jailor, Lady Gimcrack; and marriage is their sole escape. Lust does not tempt them, as it does Lady Gimcrack who, during the masquerade in Act V, manages to seduce first Bruce and then Longvil in her private rooms. She disguises herself as Miranda and Clarinda, so that the rakes are exposed to further criticism since the girls they love *are* virtuous. The seduction also points up the men's essential blindness in courtship. Clarinda and Miranda are not adverse to loving, but they control their passions, hoarding them for the husband who will free them from the familial tyrant. The girls triumph, but—unlike Lady Gimcrack, Flirt, and Figgup—they reach their "happy ending" with doubts concerning their heroes. Lady Gimcrack is freed from the bonds of marriage, but she will continue debasing herself by keeping her paid paramour Hazard, whose real lover is Flirt. Figgup, made respectable by marriage to Snarl, will be plagued by his endless diatribes and by his desire to be soundly whipped. The girls know well that lust dominates the rakes; they do not leap swiftly into marriage, but rather move gradually into it—first, by making the men their legal guardians; and, secondly, after a time in which their loyalty will be tested, perhaps by making them their husbands.

Only Sir Samuel remains uncommitted to romance or marriage. He will go on to indulge his boyish "humor" for pranks, irrelevant masquerading, farcical beatings—and for love-making which will never be consummated. He remains free, but his precious freedom is absurd. Freedom or commitment, which is ultimately best? Shadwell is unwilling to tell us.

Although Shadwell approaches in *Epsom-Wells* and *The Virtuoso* the comic mode from two directions, the witty and the humorous, in both plays he develops much the same kinds of comic action and types of character which appear in all of his comedies. Both plays are linked by a common theme, treated differently: that much defined and enigmatic term, nature. Nature in *Epsom* is the world close to the soil, flowing with the waters of the earth and unalloyed by the geegaws of civilization. Nature in *The Virtuoso* is nature misunderstood, a secret force which scientists and lovers seek to control but which remains forever outside their power.

CHAPTER 4

Triumphant Women

ETWEEN 1678 and 1681, Shadwell provided the Duke's
Company at Dorset Garden with three comedies in which
he explored most elaborately a motive recurrent in all of his
comedies: the place of the female in a comic world and the manner in which she achieves her triumph. The titles indicate this
"female focus," and the plays themselves form a specific unit in
the Shadwell canon. *A True Widow* traces the criminal career of
Lady Cheatly and treats the female motive with satiric and
complex ironies reminiscent of Jonson's *The Alchemist. The
Woman-Captain* approaches the motive farcically; a drama
without a hero, its female figure assumes the roles of both hero
and heroine in a society dominated by fops and coxcombs. *The
Lancashire Witches* blends together farcical witchcraft and witty
romance, fantasy and "realism," in a dramatic delineation of the
figurative and literal demoniac nature of women.

The idea of triumphant women was not new in Shadwell's
comedies. Except for the singular example of Lady Loveyouth
in *The Humorists,* all of Shadwell's women (whether promiscuous or innocent, silly or wise, malicious or tender) triumph in
a world presumably dominated by the male. Each of these
women possesses a remarkable talent for assessing the ways of
the world, for perceiving the weaknesses of her hero and the
strategy of her rivals and enemies, for choosing swiftly the surest
course of action, and for manipulating events so that she can
reach her happy end. Her triumph is marriage, the crowning
prize. The low female, the bawd or servant, using the flimsiest
of disguises and tricks, dupes her coxcomb into wedlock. A hero
is too wise to be fooled by a bawd, but not by the heroine who
guides, cajoles, converts him into a fiancé or groom.

Even on the rare occasions when a woman is denied her marriage wish, her loss is paradoxically her gain. Mrs. Striker fails
to win Crazy in *The Humorists,* but she is preserved from a

grim denouement as the wife of a venereally diseased husband. Shadwell's men rarely triumph, and their efforts are often punished rather than rewarded. Coxcombs are doomed to wives they hate. Bullies are incarcerated while their partners in adultery are forgiven by hypocritical cuckolds. Wise rakes, who are definitively anti-matrimonialist, discover, before the comedy ends, that passion has hurled them into marriage and that freedom is the price they must pay.

Many of the female triumphs are, however, ironic; and, from a moral standpoint, they are not victories. A low female improves her social and financial position through marriage, but she dooms herself and her groom to a life freighted with *ennui* and dislike. She achieves no recognitions of value; she simply confirms her suspicions that men are easily duped. She is metamorphosed from deceitful bawd to deceitful bride, and her marriage, we are led to understand, will be a perpetual commitment to deception. But the heroine's triumph is far less ironic (or in a different, more subtle way) and not morally objectionable. Although she feels just as surely as the bawd the lure of the flesh and although she employs equally felicitous disguises, she surrenders neither her dearly guarded virtue nor her integrity.

Pugenello's malice informs her love-strategy, however, for she often regards herself as a commercial agent bartering her chastity, beauty, and wit for the hero's freedom. According to her recurrent imagery, courtship is a commercial event and she satirically debases the elevated language in which the rake tends to couch his passion. Ironic-comic parallels existing between heroines and low females are, however, always subject to qualification—that is, a heroine may "trade" on her virtue in a commercially oriented society, but what she has to give *is* valuable in a society where virtue is scarce. To stoop to the bawd's position of marketing cheaply her womanhood would be out of the question for her, not only because her rake would never marry an unchaste woman but because she seriously cherishes the ideal of chastity.

And, even though marriage to an ex-rake hardly assures her of a life of happiness, she knows that, in an absurd world, she has won a rare, reformable creature—the handsome, wealthy, witty man. To the low female, marriage is a socio-ecclesiastical device for rising on the socio-economic ladder and for assuming a protective, official respectability, while unofficially she may commit adultery behind her dull husband's back. Despite the heroine's frequent protestations to the contrary, she affirms the traditional, sacred, and stabilizing function of marriage, the submission of male and female in a meaningful compact. The value of her triumph is ultimately moral as well as social.

I The Lady As Criminal

A True Widow utilizes several techniques, symbols, and themes reminiscent of Shadwell's earlier plays; but they are subsumed skillfully under the comedy's central metaphors—the art of cheating and of creating illusions, and the distinctions between conscious and unconscious pretension.[1] The principal character is Lady Cheatly, the unscrupulous widow of the title and the "humors"-center around which the duped characters revolve. Lady Cheatly has come to London for three reasons: to amass a fortune, to marry off her two daughters, and to marry herself to a prosperous man. This money-marriage quest is tinged by bitterness and by pathos, in the casual reference to an unscrupulous brother-in-law who robbed her of her late husband's entire estate. We are led to believe that, before she lost her wealth, she was a fine aristocrat; but that chaotic familial-financial relationships, recalling those in *The Miser,* compelled the emergence of an incipient criminality and an innate feminine ruthlessness which could save her and her daughters from the grim realities of poverty.

To gain her three ends, Lady Cheatly poses as a wealthy, commercially reliable "banker" in order to lure to her home London merchants who entrust their money to her. But she embezzles their money by having the parties concerned sign legal documents with disappearing ink. Her villainy is not restricted to the merchants; it also extends to members of her family and her staff. For example, she transforms an honest steward into her confederate in crime because he loves her and gladly sacrifices his integrity for her. When she refuses to requite his love, he threatens to expose her; she retaliates by shanghaiing him; when this fails, she tricks him into a mock-marriage; finally, remorselessly, she turns him over to the law as the scapegoat for her crimes.

In the case of her daughters (Isabella, "a Woman of Wit and Vertue," and Gartrude, a "very foolish and whorish" girl), she invites to her establishment in Act II the verbose Lady Busy, an aristocrat whose perverted "humor" is to play a fashionable procuress. Lady Busy thinks it "fit the Young should submit themselves to the gravity and discretion of the Old"—which means that they should abandon all hope of trapping an eligible fiancé in an age when married love is no longer à la mode. Fashion dictates morality; promiscuous love is not, therefore, a sin; being a mistress is the wisest course of action, "for do not Ladies of Wit and Honour, keep dayly Company" with London bachelors. Her axioms are comically perverted: "as long as you are true to one Man, Madam, you are in a manner his Lady, I say in a manner his Lady, 'tis a kind of Marriage, and great Persons most commonly cohabit longer with Mistresses, than they used to do with Wives." Lady Cheatly agrees with Lady Busy who titillates Gartrude's lust but repels the morally sensitive Isabella. Before the comedy ends, Gartrude enjoys promiscuous love; like Isabella, she also wins a husband; and their mother manages to pluck for herself a husband, the shrewd merchant Maggott, from the parade of suitors who troop to her house. Lady Cheatly gains her three ends in a society which, as the play suggests, is peculiarly adapted for the success of villains, particularly female villains.

But Lady Cheatly is not merely a one-dimensional villain; unscrupulous, embittered, determined, intelligent, she is above all a powerful character, melodramatic to some extent and, despite her immorality, never a fool. Alone in a predatory world, she sees others with psychological penetration and employs consciously, even artistically, her methods to dupe those persons clearly born to be duped. This role makes her a critic of society who, like Jonson's ironic satirists Face and Volpone, has learned to live in a world where deception and self-deception are the rule. She never deceives herself and she is never (unlike the dupes) blind to her own failings. Thus she differs from Lady Busy who is villain and fool. Lady Cheatly's great strength resides in her shrewd appreciation of distinctions between appearance and reality and in her power to use both for her own ends. This ability, which leads to her triumph, also ironically is the source of triumph of the virtuous characters, particularly of the hero, Carlos. He alone is shrewd enough to compete with Lady Cheatly in deception. And, although they never come into direct conflict with each other, they are implicitly contrasted throughout the entire play.

When the comedy begins, we learn that Carlos has recently returned from the Continent. Unlike the typical rake, he found the Grand Tour a dismal bore. His adventures have convinced him of one thing only—that he should wed Theodosia, a girl whom he has known for some time. Whereas Lady Cheatly is the first instance in Shadwell of the seriously criminal "humors" character, Carlos is the first instance of the seriously reforming rake who surely and sincerely professes his love. Both types were to appear with greater frequency in Shadwell's later comedies, but in A True Widow they are full-blooded embodiments of two extremes in the appearance-reality motive. Lady Cheatly is false within, but she triumphs by artful appearances and goes unpunished for her immorality; Carlos is true within, but, because Theodosia suspects his honesty, she *demands* that he enact the part of a frivolous gallant. By the strange circumstances of the comic world in which they function, Lady Cheatly and Carlos must appear to be what they are not in order to arrive at their happy endings.

Theodosia is a cleverly conceived "inversion" of the usual Restoration comic heroine. Typically, she doubts the hero's protestations of eternal passion, but most untypically her doubts are ill founded. Instead of trying to reform Carlos (which she has no need to do) she insists that he make all of the women in the play fall in love with him. It is strange, indeed, to observe the lusty beau objecting to her frivolous test which most of Shadwell's heroes would have welcomed. And yet her test is not, as Carlos imagines, so frivolous. Actually, she wishes to press him to the brink of a love affair, of several love affairs, with women she knows, and then, of course, to make certain that he remains untempted and true to her. Given *carte blanche* to woo and finally managing to make all of the women respond to him, Carlos yet refuses them and confirms the absolute reality of his honest wit and moral wisdom—the two qualities which firmly separate him from the other characters, particularly from Lady Cheatly.

His wit and wisdom are set forth in the opening scene. In

dialogues with his friend Bellamour and with another shrewd
libertine Stanmore, and then later with the trio of coxcombs
(foppish Selfish, poetaster Young Maggot, and sportsman Prig),
Carlos tells of his newly discovered views of love and marriage
in a world where pretense is rampant and appearance is commonly accepted as reality. Indicting specifically society's various
"humors," he singles out Stanmore as a perfect example. Stanmore is a wit whose genteel relationships with lovers and friends
are mere shams to hide a feverish lust that controls his will and
is the center and totality of his being. He is not what he says
and thinks he is, a gallant. He is a "loving Rogue," not "good
for any thing." Carlos looks for those individual ruling passions
everywhere that he goes. And his diatribes set the stage for our
impressions of the characters of the comedy, particularly of the
three "humors" who appear in this opening scene.

Selfish is an amorist, suffering from delusions of narcissism;
the only girl with whom he can fall in love is Gartrude Cheatly,
because they look alike, because she is the mirror of his *soi-
disant* beauty. Maggot, the law-student and would-be poet and
rebel against the crass commercialism of his Uncle Maggot, is
really a cowardly, uninspired dunce who aspires zealously to the
mysteries of art but is incapable even of concealing his ignorance
or of creating the "illusion" for the world that he *is* an artist.
(One thinks of Ninny in *The Sullen Lovers*.) Lady Cheatly and
Carlos are the true artists of the play, although neither professes
to be an artist. With a surer talent than the untalented Maggot,
they fabricate for public consumption convincing illusions of
themselves as honest widow and lubricious rake. Young Maggot
must also be compared to Prig, a man appalled by art, who
dwells in a child's world and finds joy only in sports. Prig is a
"masculine" fool; Young Maggot is a "feminine" fool, and this
difference between them is sharply established in their singing
competition.

Maggot's pastoral, "Damon *see how charming* Chloris," reflects his banal sense of passion; Prig's *"One Night Walking in a
Wood,"* a crude tavern song, tells of his bluntly carnal interest
in women. These men and their songs represent dramatically the
two extremes between which Carlos stands. Carlos idealizes his
perfect "Chloris," but without banality; he knows that carnality
informs (but does not dominate) his love. Only Bellamour,

Isabella's pursuer, approximates Carlos in this matter of loving; and Carlos admires him because he can turn a "lustful humor" into a deeper love.

After the three gallants and three fools, Shadwell draws our attention to Lady Cheatly and to her home where (for the remainder of Acts I, II, III, and V) we find ourselves in an atmosphere of deception with the hostess as arch-deceiver. We find her explaining to her Cousin Lump, a mercenary Puritan, why she has come to London, and she then prepares her dinner party for the suitors. The party (Acts II and III) is punctuated by varieties of duplicity—from the hostess' sordid business transactions to Poet Maggot's hopeless efforts to woo Isabella. At the invitation of Carlos (he is there to woo Isabella's closest friend, Theodosia), the party-guests go off to the theater. In Act IV, which takes place *in* the playhouse, Shadwell projects symbolically and in literal theatrical terms the appearance-reality motive. The theater-within-the-theater scene creates a lucid center (apart from that other "theater," Lady Cheatly's) where deceptions and self-deceptions are proliferated into a complex statement about the relation between *comic* pretense and *artistic* illusion.[2]

Three distinct sets of characters appear in the playhouse scene: (i) the dinner guests—the characters who have occupied the stage for the first three acts; (ii) several rowdy theatergoers, rude gallants, critics, and ladies who, pushing their way into the theater without paying (on "tick"), damn *a priori* the play by Mr. Prickett and disturb everyone; (iii) the actors, anxious to please but stifled by Prickett's dull farce. The play-within-the play tells of two rakes who hide, one after the other, beneath a table when the husband they have been cuckolding disrupts their rendezvous with his wife.

The play is important to the central meaning of *A True Widow* because it illustrates the failure to create a satisfactory dramatic illusion. Language and action, what the characters say and what they do, are uncorrelated: the florid style, coupled with slapstick farce, shatters the necessary absolute liaison between dialogue and plot which creates, in any dramatic work, the illusion of a reality. One lover, merely animalistic in his purpose, philosophizes inanely: he tells the wife that "since Fortune (by so many frequent Signalizations) has demonstrated how much she is a friend to us, . . . it will be a hainous tergiversation from her, to abandon that trust we formerly have reposed in her, and she may justly take a Picque at our infidelity, and, in that Caprice, may contrive a revenge sutable to our delinquency." This dialogue, a parody of the language of witty love-making, which Theodosia calls "lewd Stuff" and Young Maggot "strong, sinewy, and correct Style," gives way to farce when the wife fails to convince her husband that the two male shapes who flee in the dark are devils. The scuffling on stage between cuckold and lovers gives way in turn to a brawl in the audience when sportsman Prig strikes one of the rowdies. Carlos is superficially wounded, which brings to a climax Theodosia's test; all the ladies (Isabella, Gartrude, Lady Busy, and Lady Cheatly) surround him, consoling the wounded "hero" and expressing, if not passion, at least some affection for him.

The brawl has other comic effects. It flusters the actors who leave the theater—one actress, perhaps the one who played the wife, "being frighted with the Swords, is fallen into a Fit, and carried home sick." Yet Carlos, feeling responsible for the theater party, announces his intention to take over the playhouse and to provide the entertainment. Aware that the characters of *A True Widow* make better comic fools as "real" persons than Prickett's unlikely characters, he assumes literally the role of "theatrical director" manipulating *his* players in a series of broadly comic scenes. As audience, we switch attention from the triteness of Prickett's farce to the real farce: Shadwell's and Carlos' comic world. On the stage within the stage, in the pit, behind the scenes, all the characters of the play are seen to incorporate themselves irrevocably into *their* comedy, revealing themselves on the "stage" of the world. This is the "real" entertainment, far more meaningful and humorous than the uninspired farce of adultery and dissimulation which barely touched the heart of the idea of deception and pretense, the great comic theme of *A True Widow*.

Carlos and, to a lesser degree, Lady Cheatly control the second entertainment, acting their parts in the comedy but still remaining detached, the mocking spectators of it. Behind the scenes without Carlos' aid, Selfish and then Stanmore seduce the masked Gartrude believing her to be Isabella. The enraged Bellamour, also mistaking Gartrude for Isabella, castigates her when he thinks he sees her fornicating with Selfish; he thereby exposes his inability to perceive the great difference between Isabella's actual virtue and her lewd sister's thin disguise. These symbolic, behind-the-scenes entertainments bring to the surface Gartrude's sheer lubricity, the lust of Selfish and Stanmore, and Bellamour's weak faith.

Carlos prepares specific on-the-stage entertainment in which other crucial revelations are made. First he calls for a dance of professional clowns; their pantomime is a Pugenello-like comment on the general atmosphere of malice and folly informing the lives of the dinner guests. Lady Cheatly arranges with a Stage Carpenter to prepare "machines" which will carry up and away some of her dunces. While Puritan Lump, the first victim, expiates on modern vice, two mock-devils carry him up, punishing him appropriately for his hypocritical zeal and pride. Young Maggot then recites a poem ("Beauty, thou great preserver of the World./By which into dead Lumps quick life is hurl'd"), while Prig rails at the versifier. Lady Cheatly answers them by having them *carried up in their Chairs, and hang in the Air,* where they symbolically belong.

This masterly act ends, however, on a note of impending disaster for Lady Cheatly. Gartrude's promiscuity (like her Steward's revolt) threatens the success of her programme. Gartrude, by losing her maidenhead, has lost her market-value as a bride, and the danger of imprisonment becomes apparent. In Act V, Lady Cheatly's "actors" and her "plots" start moving out of her control, yet it is a tribute to her shrewdness as a puppeteer that she tricks Young Maggot into marrying Gartrude, makes the Steward pay for her crimes, and takes a husband for herself. A cunning businessman, Old Maggot learns of her embezzling, seems to admire her for it, and hints that he will join her in crime. A third marriage agreement follows when Bellamour and Isabella settle their differences and reach lovingly the "Inn of Matrimony."

Only Theodosia persists as the unmoved female, declaiming against the "Plague of Marriage" which rages in the house. Although Carlos has passed her test and should, by agreement, win her, she remains the inveterate doubter. All his art and honesty have not convinced her to differentiate between what he is and what she fears he is, an incorrigible rake. Isabella per-

suades her to share in the comic ending; and, like the girls in
Epsom-Wells and *The Virtuoso*, Theodosia puts Carlos on proba-
tion—but only for a month. Their denouement should be contrasted to the Stanmore-Selfish denouement. These men, having
deflowered Gartrude, satisfy their lust without penalty of marriage; and Gartrude clearly hints that, as Mrs. Maggot, she will
be available to them at their bidding. The untrammeled
bachelorhood of these males seems shallow indeed compared to
Carlos' romantic expectations of enjoying a life less lonely, a
journey more tolerable with his wiser, wittier Theodosia. In a
world so farcical and frivolous, so deceitful and witless, such a
conclusion is a triumph indeed.

II *The Lady As Man*

The poor reception of *A True Widow* encouraged Shadwell to
give his audiences something they would better appreciate, low
farce—or so he remarked with indignant tone in his Epilogue
to the farcial *The Woman-Captain:*

> *He found by's last, you would not like what's good,*
> *Though it was praised by all that understood.*
> *Remembering how you used that last he writ,*
> *He made this Low, so to your Level fit;*
> *Plenty of Noise, and scarcity of Wit. . . .*

He abandoned, indeed, in this comedy, the intricate symbolic-
dramatic patterns of *A True Widow* and provided instead a com-
paratively elemental study of the triumphant female. This bald,
direct treatment, which he considered the crux of farce, is not
however without typical Shadwellian ironies.

There is no hero in *The Woman-Captain;* or, put another way,
there is a Mrs. Gripe who, unable to find a hero in decadent
London, learns to become her *own* hero. Her problem is plainly
set forth: married to an old usurer who does not satisfy her in
any way and who keeps her imprisoned (as Corvino keeps Celia
in *Volpone*), she resolves on a plan of deception to regain her
freedom.[3] She dons a soldier's uniform, poses as her soldier-
brother, and (assisted by her brother's corporal) she wages a
war against Old Gripe. Through tricks and threats she finally

crushes his tyrannic spirit as well as the spirits of a band of bullies who surround the would-be hero, Sir Humphrey Scattergood. Mrs. Gripe is Shadwell's most amazonian heroine; her aggressiveness inspires the slapstick madness of a topsy-turvy world where a woman must become a man and make most of the men in the play cower like frightened women.

Sir Humphrey is Shadwell's most notorious rake—aside from the demonic Don John of *The Libertine*. John is a tragic study of inordinate naturalistic iconoclasm; Sir Humphrey is a comic study of libertinism reduced to a social-psychological absurdity. Sir Humphrey is also a comic version of the tragic Timon; he is an extravagant prodigal who loses within a few hours his estate, his so-called friends, and his bachelorhood when he marries his courtesan to whom (in a fit of generosity) he signed over his entire wealth. The movement of the action is dependent on his fall as well as on the contrasting, parallel action of Mrs. Gripe's rise. His defeat and her victory stem from a similar cause, however, for both of them are revolting against restrictions imposed by older, familial tyrants. The rake's father restricted him excessively.

The play occurs on Sir Humphrey's birthday, when he comes of age after his father's death; and, overwhelmed by his new freedom and financial power, he goes "mad." He dedicates himself to an active, total rejection of the past and plans, it seems, to turn his life into one continuous birthday party. He dismisses his father's Fool (an unnecessary character in the modern age when there are so many unprofessional fools to amuse him), supplies prostitutes for his companions, forces his father's faithful and moral retainer to indulge in distasteful fornication, and lavishes expensive gifts on everyone. In contrast, Mrs. Gripe must *find* her freedom which she values no less than he but which she realizes is precious, "fragile." He wastes it capriciously; she gains it cautiously. A tribute to her clever strategies is that her quest ends in victory, and an indictment of his folly that his quest leads to disaster.

Two important themes are unfolded in the process of Sir Humphrey's fall and Mrs. Gripe's rise. The first concerns a problem which Shadwell was to emphasize in his late comedies, particularly in *The Squire of Alsatia*, but which, in *The Woman-Captain*, he develops as an overtone. Sir Humphrey is not alone responsible for his fall; the responsibility rests, in good part, with his father and a restrictive upbringing where the claims of natural passion, of youth's self-indulgent propensities, were denied. This educational theme is echoed in Mrs. Gripe's reasons for revolution; the restrictive life imposed by her stingy husband is suggestive of another failure of the age to answer the claims of youthful freedom—not, in Mrs. Gripe's case, promiscuity, but the right to live a sane, married existence without perpetual, meaningless suspicion. Her relationship with Gripe teaches her the significance of freedom. In her simple way, she learns through personal suffering the meaning of tyranny. She turns the world upside-down, rejecting publicly her female role, turning herself (unnaturally) into a male and becoming her own hero in a society which seems able to produce nothing but selfish weaklings.

The second important theme, one which runs through all of Shadwell's plays, is that of social leveling. Sir Humphrey not only rejects the past *in toto* but fails to preserve a meaningful future for his class. His fall ends with the rise of Phillis, a whore, to the English aristocracy. Her triumph points up symbolically the degeneration of the English male and of the older aristocracy which did not provide a firm basis for existence for its offspring. The Sir Humphreys have become boy-men, dependent upon whores to pay their way through life. Mrs. Gripe's victory is a finer one: quitting her defeated husband and her old life, she launches forth on a new life taking her marriage portion and her virtue with her.

III   *The Lady As Witch*

The Lancashire Witches, and Tegue O Divelly the Irish Priest is set "in *Lancashire,* near *Pendle-Hills*" shortly after the famous Popish Plot of 1678; but some of its characters, in particular its witches, are modeled after persons involved in the English witchcraft trials of 1612 and 1633, trials which served as the basis for Heywood and Brome's *The Late Lancashire Witches* produced in 1634.[4] In this country setting, far removed from London's drawingrooms, taverns, parks, and theaters, Shadwell creates an atmosphere which is implicitly and often ironically compared and contrasted to London's atmosphere. The techniques are similar to those of *Epsom-Wells* and of the later *Bury-Fair*. Restoration attitudes toward country life and folk were ambiguous, and Shadwell exploits this ambiguity in his comic treatment of triumphant women and defeated men in this play.

On the one hand, Shadwell conventionally regards the country as a place by no means exempt from the debilitating debauchery of city folk; crass rather than genteel in their pleasures, country folk share the universal potential for folly and sin. The differences are largely matters of style. The country then is not the true locale of an idealized pastoralism nor a romantic sanctuary where spiritual and emotional health is possible. On the other hand, the age saw the country as a place where a good degree of freedom, peace, and quiet could be obtained; it was far enough away from the distractions and noises of overcivilized London life. Shadwell's great tribute to rural life is made by Bellamy in *Bury-Fair*. In *The Lancashire Witches*, Shadwell shows us that country life is proper for an intelligent country squire who equally abhors rural vulgarity and citified foppery. Sir Edward Hartfort, the *raissonneur* father of the mischievous heroine in whose house most of the action occurs, is "A worthy Hospitable true English Gentleman, of good understanding, and honest Principles." He stands in contradistinction to his superstitious, dull-witted neighbor, Sir Jeffrey Shacklehead, and to several other Lancashire clods, the typical targets of satire on country people and manners.

The comedy is about two rakes who come to Lancashire in pursuit of Sir Edward's daughter, Isabella, and Sir Jeffrey's daughter, Theodosia. The rakes recognize instantly the intellectual sanctity of Hartfort's world, particularly of his fine estate which is emblematic of his wisdom and virtue. After a tour of the grounds, young Bellfort eulogizes in Act III: "Methinks you represent to us the Golden days of Queen *Elizabeth*, such sure were our Gentry then; now they are grown servile Apes to foreign customes, they leave off Hospitality, for which We were famous all over *Europe*, and turn Servants to Board-wages." As an idealized member of the true gentry, Sir Edward sustains the traditional paternalism of the aristocratic ideal; his Elizabethan virtues are, of course, implicitly contrasted to modern Caroline failings. Bellfort and his friend Doubty join the father in various patriotic effusions on England's isolationism, its monarchial ideals, its religion, and its heroines ("Women of good Humour, Wit, and Beauty"). Sir Edward's estate is not only the emblem of an English historical ideal; it is also the emblem of a Classical-Christian ideal, the Golden Age. Its garden is a paradise which, according to Theodosia, "affords variety of Pleasures; nothing here is wanting." Yet these prelapsarian descriptions of the place and of its demi-god squire undergo severe, comic qualifications; for the comedy (a satire on rationalism as well as on superstition) subjects this perfect Hartfortian universe to various kinds of ironic examinations.

At the heart of this universe is Sir Edward's rationalistic philosophy. He scoffs, of course, at the credulous Sir Jeffrey who is in hot pursuit of local witches. Yet there really are local witches; and, most ironically, they congregate in Sir Edward's cellar. The integrity of the English paradise-on-earth is threatened also in other ways. His son and heir is "A Clownish, sordid" oaf who idealizes but two things, ale-drinking and hunting. His only daughter he has affianced to young Sir Timothy Shackle-head. This young man is a fop, a clown à la mode, adored by a doting mother who took charge of his education, sent him to Oxford and to the Inns-of-Court, bought him a knighthood, and is firmly convinced that she has produced a gallant of the first order.

Into Edward's estate flock other fools and villains. Smerk, the Anglican clergyman attached to the Hartfort family, is a hypo-crite who wants to gain spiritual power over Hartfort's servants and family. He has an eye on Isabella and her fortune, and he is attracted to Catholic demagoguery. Perceiving this man's evil and impertinence, Sir Edward in a lengthy diatribe which opens the comedy and which Shadwell was forced to excise from the stage production, rails against upstarts, hypocrites, and fools, establishing clearly for Smerk his ideals of family life, of action, of character and, above all, of the place of religion in modern life. Religion is a tool for rational living, not a device for men like Smerk to climb the social ladder. Sir Edward, remembering doubtlessly the years of bloody religious wars, sternly warns him: *"Search not the secrets of my House or me," "Preach nothing but good life and honesty."*

But his position as the ideal parent-monarch is violated also by Isabella who refuses to marry Sir Timothy but who is also unwilling to disobey her father. Surreptitiously, she plans to disrupt his plans for her marriage. She will turn Sir Timothy against her and so be free to choose her own husband. Appreciative in all other respects of her father's wisdom, she wonders at his remarkable failure to realize how poor a marriage he has arranged. The logic behind his illogical match is an economic-patriotic one: the Shacklehead estate and the Hartfort estate will be merged and solidified.

Against the arch-invaders of his paradise (the real witches and the unprincipled Irish priest Father Kelly, alias Tegue, who is invited by the Shackleheads to exorcise the witches), Sir Edward's wisdom and virtue are unimpeachable. He never personally encounters the witches or the Devil himself who presides over their black Sabbath in the shape of a buck-goat, but he clashes head on with the irrational voluptuary Tegue, as do all the wise people of the play. Tegue is the great offender of Edward's paradise, and at the end of Act V we are shown that he is an overt threat to the English throne and church. A leading figure in the scandalous Popish Plot, a foreign destructive force come to England to breed hate and chaos, he is an "equal mixture of Fool and Knave," a dangerous and silly demon.[5] Tegue represents Shadwell's ever-growing effort to incorporate into his comic-"humors" world scoundrels who seriously endanger society, but whose knavery is so blatant that they emerge ultimately as mere buffoons.

The *Witches* is concerned primarily with the ways in which women dominate men by practicing witchcraft. All the males are subjected in some way to witchcraft, real and figurative. Mother Dickenson tricks Tegue into an act of fornication; Mal Spencer possesses her love, young bumpkin Clod; the maid Susan uses a magic potion to turn cold Smerk into her frenzied lover and, finally, husband; even the witch-hunter Lady Shacklehead, although her lusty pursuit of Bellfort and Doubty fails, uses the excuse of bewitchment to convince her dull-witted husband that she is faithful.

Isabella and Theodosia practice the black art in its more subtle, comic forms. The traditional analogies between charming, devilish girls and *real* female servants of Lucifer are expressed both metaphorically and literally. The girls charm "unreformable" rakes into honest husbands. They break legal obligations to marry unworthy husbands (Theodosia is also committed to marry a man she hates, Young Hartfort). They drive their fiancés to distraction by their pranks, and in Act V they literally don witches' costumes and confuse the entire household. Their darkest crime is their disobedience of their parents, for they wed the rakes without parental consent. In this disobedience they are intimately allied to the "Old Serpent" Satan and reenact man's original transgression. But they practice witchcraft in the name of love and liberty and as a criticism of an obstructive paternalistic order. Mother Dickenson, Mal Spencer, and the other real witches have already given the Devil their bodies and souls and are committed to throw the peaceful world of Lancashire into utter chaos. In "miniature" fashion, Isabella and Theodosia also bend their talents to create havoc in Sir Edward's otherwise rationally ordered universe. In the paradisal context of his estate they enact a comic second fall.

Specific allusions to witchcraft, frequent in the action, usually indicate the value of employing black magic to achieve one's ends when ordinary methods prove useless. Isabella obviously loathes Sir Timothy, yet he calls her coldness an expression of affection, and he sees her as "the pretty witch that enchants my heart." First she attacks him verbally, then physically by hurling stones, and then she lies to her father by insisting, like a naughty child, on her innocence. Tim only imagined her malice; "sure, . . . he is bewitched." Theodosia is her confederate in lying. Perjuriously she swears that witches inhabit the house (they actually do) and are causing Tim's confusion. She herself uses witchcraft to ward off Young Hartfort, an uninspired groom. Wives to him are useful for one thing—to protect a man against witches at night. In Act II, after some hopeless efforts to bring himself up to wooing the girl he is to marry the following morning, he falls asleep in a chair; mischievous Theodosia, largely to terrify him, pulls the chair out from under him. Her prank is a witch's prank—or so it is to superstitious Hartfort who awakens from a dream about witches and cries for help against the "vanished" witch. But these attempts to turn Tim and Hartfort against them all meet with failure. The girls find themselves in a desperate situation by Acts IV and V, which begin in the dead of night and end on the following morning when their forced marriages are scheduled to take place.

It is in Act IV that they resolve definitely to deny parental decrees. They will marry their heroes. They have already charmed them, but under ordinary circumstances they would less immodestly delay their courtship and wedding. Time presses, however, and the rakes, calling their witches "Angels," demand a secret marriage before daybreak. Act IV, scene iii, inaugurates a series of farcical confusions. First the girls hide in the rakes' rooms, but are quickly dispatched because Sir Jeffrey comes, thinking that they are witches roaming about the house. Lady Shacklehead, en route to Doubty's bedroom in the dark, finds herself abandoned by him and then attacked by lecherous Tegue. She evades the priest who erroneously fornicates with Mother Dickenson believing her to be Lady Shacklehead. His horror over "Copulaation too vid a Succubus," spoken in the Irish dialect that distinguishes his language, epitomizes the comic grotesqueness of his character; and Mother Dickenson (in *her* lecherous way) becomes his most powerful critic. Sir Jeffrey soon discovers his half-naked wife roaming in the darkness. Like the girls, she uses witchcraft to excuse her compromising situation: "Oh! the Witch, the Witch, oh she pulls the cloaths off me. Hold me, Sir *Jeffrey*, hold me," feigning sonambulism and deceiving her gullible lord.

In the final act, as a climax to the implicit parallels between feminine mischief and true sorcery, Isabella and Theodosia disguise themselves as witches in a last ditch attempt to ward off the dull fiancés. After terrifying Susan, Smerk, and Tegue, the four lovers find themselves briefly alone. Tim appears, observing them in horror and overhearing Bellfort woo Theodosia ("A Thousand blessings light on thee, my Dear Pretty Witch"), comes very close to the figurative truth when he calls Bellfort "the Devil" in his traditional posture of "Courting of a Witch." The girls' disguises send everyone in false directions—except the two gay couples. Witchcraft having capped their triumphs, they marry the men; and, when the girls finally announce the event to their parents, the whole suggestion of the second fall is sharply etched. The girls are eternal Eves. The men are more Adam than Devil in asking for the fathers' forgiveness.

All of these comic-romantic incidents are linked to a darker

kind of witchcraft which has as its purpose a serious destruction
of familial-social relations and the creation of chaos. Through
witchcraft, Smerk gives up his social climbing and finds Susan
overwhelmingly desirable. Through witchcraft but without love
potions, pretty girls ally themselves to devils and destroy the
laws of Sir Edward and Sir Jeffrey. But these triumphs are
directly and indirectly brought about by Mother Dickenson and
her haggish crew. They create storms, make candles fly through
the air, turn men into horses and ride on them through the sky,
transform themselves into rabbits and cats; they confuse, in short,
all superstitious Lancashire folk who blame everything unusual
that happens on them. Their first storm brings the four lovers
together. Bellfort and Doubty, in a sense bewitched before the
comedy opens at a spa where they met the girls some months before, are traveling through the countryside in search of the
Hartfort estate. They are about to bypass it when, because of
the witches' storm, they are forced to take shelter under a tree
upon which Clod is sitting, placed there by the prankish witches.
Without a storm, the rakes would not have arrived at the estate
until the following day, too late to prevent the forced marriages.
In the last two acts, the haggish crew not only prevents Tegue's
rape of Lady Shacklehead, but it provides (in its chaos) a
figurative smoke screen for the harassed couples. But above all
the witches emphasize the differences between Hartfort's orderly
world and their disharmonious world.

In Act IV, for example, Sir Edward entertains his guests with
a concert of fine music—for Shadwell, an image of the intelligent
harmony which this wise rural lord embodies—but the witches
cause the instruments to go out of control. Music becomes noise
that shatters and defies his harmonious powers. Most of the
witches' acts are mere pranks meant solely to frighten gullible
country persons, good-natured "Horatian" satire. But often the
acts reveal a deeper sense of the macabre, of death, and the
Devil. One of the hags, in the shape of a bird, is shot in flight,
her wing blown off; and, when she reassumes her human shape,
she is monstrously minus a limb. The Inquisition scene (where
stupefied Lancashire bumpkins testify to the horrors perpetrated
by the hags) heightens by quasi-ridiculous, quasi-sinister illustrations their demoniac potential. Shadwell does not wish to suggest that witchcraft exists solely in the minds of superstitious

people; his aim is to undercut Sir Edward's safe and rational view of life.

This objective is especially true of the scenes in Sir Edward's cellar where the witches perform for their lover, the Devil. While they allow us to recognize that the squire is needlessly proud of his rationalism, they also show us a grotesqueness which is hardly comic. The hags express a primordial essence of sin, destruction, and horror. They are bent on dismembering the body social, for their terrors extend beyond the confines of their own authentic commitment to Lucifer and into the world of honest men, beasts, plants, and places. When in Act II the Devil asks them to report their latest accomplishments, what they have "done for my delight?/Relate the service of the night," each tells of her adventures in chaos—of the sucking of the breath and blood of an unchristened child, of the amassing of dead men's flesh and bones, and of the "glewy Stuff" they collect from corpses' eyes:

> Their Eye-balls with my nailes scoop'd out,
> And pieces of their Limbs I've brought—
> A Brat ith' Mothers Womb I slew:
> The Fathers neck I twisted too.

The antimasque elements of the scene are iterated in an elaborate initiation sequence in Act III where contrasts are suggested between the adoration of Lucifer by the proselyte Madge and the courtship of the gay couples. Appropriately, the action takes place "Within this Shattered Abby Walls." The Devil enumerates for Madge the cardinal rules of witchcraft in a black sacrament. She must renounce Heaven; she must perform many pranks and minor cruelties; she "must each month some murdered Children pay." Above all, she must perpetually *"Curse Heaven, Plague Mankind"* before she may *"go forth and be a Witch."* An elaborate five-part song ending in a dance *"with fantastick unusual postures"* makes clear that the Devil's power is eternally destructive and obscene and that it is opposed for-ever to the divine-rationalism of Sir Edward:

> *O're Nature's Powers thou canst prevail,*
> *Raise Winds, bring Snow, or Rain, or Hail,*
> *Without their Causes, and canst make*
> *The steady Course of Nature shake.*

[94]

In the mysterious life of demons and of lovely ladies, Sir Edward's enlightenment does not apply. The wits in *The Virtuoso* would have held that Sir Edward lacked the Lucretian awareness of nature's ultimate strangeness. The women of the play do not lack it.

Yet Shadwell hardly invalidates the rational approach to life, for this father is contrasted to another kind of "father" and the chief butt of Shadwell's satire, Tegue "of the Devil." Tegue profits from the prevalence of witches, exploits superstition for his own ends, and presides over the farcical inquisition of the hags. His Catholicism, we see, is only a source of power for him. Through its strange rituals, he gains control of the minds of frightened fools. He employs whatever chaos exists to support a tyranny not unlike Sir Edward's over Isabella—and this is her major criticism of an otherwise excellent father. Her marriage is an act of correction; and, although Sir Edward never realizes the irrational comic and real witchcraft which led to the girls' happy endings, he swiftly comprehends the reasonableness of their choice and assents wisely to it.

The Lancashire Witches marks the end of the first phase of Shadwell's career as playwright. Before considering the remarkable comedies which signalized his return to the theater in the spring of 1688, it will be well to examine two areas of his art which have been, unfortunately, too long neglected and often unwisely disprized—his explorations into pastoral, opera and tragedy, and his poetry.

CHAPTER 5

Exploring Pastoral, Opera, and Tragedy

E VEN though Shadwell's achievements in comedy over-
shadow his efforts in pastoral, opera, and tragedy, it would
be misleading to discount as inconsequential his five adaptations
produced between 1668/9 and 1678. Apart from their historical
interest and their value as individual works of art, they provide
us with useful examples of their author's treatment of certain
favorite comic themes in different dramatic keys. The first, *The
Royal Shepherdess*, a pastoral based on John Fountain's *The
Rewards of Virtue*, was staged soon after Shadwell's first comedy.
Fountain wrote this closet drama shortly before the reopening
of the public theaters in 1660, and, apparently not expecting it
to be staged, he produced a static piece of romantic dramaturgy
based upon conventional pastoral-heroic themes. In Shadwell's
hands, the play achieves a high degree of vividness through
freshly conceived, sharply etched characterizations, swift action,
graceful lyrics, and a dialogue in blank verse which one critic
has called excellent.[1]

Shadwell's two operas—or more precisely semi-operas—represent significant milestones in the evolution of English opera;
the first is based on the Dryden-Davenant *Tempest*, the second
on the Molière-Corneille-Quinault tragedy-ballet, *Psyché*. Shortly after these unusually successful operas were produced, Shadwell tried his hand at the tragic mode with, first, *The Libertine*
(based on a play by Rosimond) and then with his version of
Shakespeare's study in misanthropy, *Timon of Athens*. *The
Libertine* introduced English theatergoers to the infamous Don
Juan, the tragic counterpart to the comic rake; his *Timon*, in-
corporating theatrical elements popular in the Restoration, held
the stage with slight variations well into the nineteenth century.
These plays, which demonstrate a versatility not often attributed

to Shadwell, are interesting, certainly adequate works, but they fall short in many ways of his achievements in the comic mode where his satiric genius flowered best.

I *Urania and the Arcadian Illusion*

The Royal Shepherdess foreshadowed the theme of triumphant women which informs the comedies treated in the previous chapter, but the theme is modified by a sentimental-pathetic tone and style peculiar to the pastoral illusion. The pastoral atmosphere is contrasted to two other atmospheres—to the heroic life of monarchs and courts and to the low life of comic villains, really "humors" characters, who express unheroic, unpastoral attitudes. Intermittently, pastoral and heroic idealism is juxtaposed to a distinctly comic view of virtue, bravery, loyalty, trust, and grand love. In so "serious" a mode as pastoral-heroic, Shadwell could not refrain from sardonic ambiguities.

Urania, the shepherdess of the title, represents pastoral perfections. After her father, the King of Thrace, died, her mother decided to preserve her from the immense sorrows of royal life by concealing her identity and by exchanging her "Scepter for a Sheep-hook." No one, except her mother, knows Urania's true identity until the final act, and so her humility coupled with her innate royalty are intended to show that she has received a perfect education as shepherdess while her essential nobility is never disguised by pastoral circumstances. The action occurs in the Arcadian Court, where, far from her humble cottage, in a glittering and corrupt civilization, Urania's woes begin.

When the Arcadian King discovers that he cannot live without her, his frenzied lust sets off a chain of chaotic events which bring Urania to the brink of death. Ironically, then, this feminine embodiment of virtue becomes unwittingly the source of the play's confusions and conflicts. She is an obstacle to the good Queen who attempts, at last successfully, to reclaim her wayward husband. Urania incites hopeless passion in Endymion, whom she rejects as lover; and Endymion's passion for her, in turn, makes the virtuous Princess Cleantha (who loves him) utterly desperate.

These confusions pave the way for three villains (foppish Neander, jealous old Geron, and his foolish wife Phronesia) who plot for power in court. They are finally exposed and appropriately exiled from Arcadia. Phronesia's fate is essentially significant as a clue to understanding Shadwell's manner of expressing the pastoral illusion. All the other women are rewarded with happy endings, except Phronesia. She must abide with her old husband; her failure is that she wed him in the first place, that she did not wisely choose her mate, the prerogative of all Shadwellian women. In the pastoral world premiums are set upon honest love and permanent unions. Phronesia's *is* permanent, but it is without the saving grace and joy which mark the multiple happy endings in the final act.

In this act Shadwell reserves the two crucial revelations which bring to an end the proliferation of crossed-loves, unrequited passions, and uncertainties that have accumulated, one by one, in the first four acts. The first revelation occurs when the King, repenting of his love for Urania, assents to the Queen's recommendation that the court pay public homage to Arcadia's national heroine, its symbol of pastoral virtue. But suddenly in the midst of the celebration, the Arcadian assembly is informed that Urania is pregnant; and the ironic reversal of tone, from the King's panegyric to his condemnation, is modified and sustained by Urania's self-defense. She reveals a truth which we half-suspected. She is the wife of Prince Theander, the King's son who has been abroad fighting Arcadia's enemies. Their marriage is clearly symbolic, perhaps allegoric, the melding of pastoral perfection and heroic greatness, of "Venus" and "Mars." But this revelation, which saves her from the embarrassments of unwed motherhood, propels her toward death; for the law decrees it a capital crime to marry an heir to the throne without official consent. As she mounts the scaffold in tears, she realizes that love can destroy her. Her mother appears to tell of her real origins, but this is insufficient reason to abrogate the law. It is Theander's triumphant return and his father's forgiveness that turn a near-tragedy into a joyous celebration of the secret marriage.

This play is not representative of Shadwell's full dramatic power, but it throws light upon his early dramatic techniques— his method of sustaining action, and here at a rapid pace compared to the slow pace of *The Sullen Lovers;* of developing ironic patterns of reversal; of suffusing the whole in a mood of delicate pastoralism, a mood so often the target of satire in his "humors" comedies. The songs show best the way in which Shadwell created the pastoral atmosphere. Fountain had written only one song, the brief *"Thus from the Prison to the Throne"* for Act V. But Shadwell added four more, two of them intricate pieces, which make up the masque for the Queen's entertainment in Act III, *"Shepherds awake, the God of day does rise"* and *"Thus all our Life long we are frolick and gay."* In their ornateness they foreshadow the spectacular masque scenes in *The Tempest* and in *Psyche*. In a second grand sequence, the celebration of Theander's victories in Act IV, a "Consort of Martial Musick" describes the great masculinity of heroic life as a natural counterpart to the tender, feminine life of pastoral; and the war music subtly reminds us of the court's destructiveness. *"All Praises to the God of War"* also foreshadows Theander's crucial appearance in Act V, but Shadwell's fourth lyric, sung in this act, evokes an utterly different mood. Sung by Arcadians, *"Lovers Lament, Lament this fatal day"* is a short dirge on the impending demise of the heroine and an ultimately ironic dirge since she is soon saved.

The Third Act masque shows how Shadwell relies on song for specific, ironic commentary on dramatic action. The Queen prepares her entertainment in the hope of obliquely and symbolically informing her husband of things which she cannot directly express—that she knows of his lust and understands it; that she wishes he will be redeemed from it and reassume his proper part as wise Arcadian king. She introduces the singers, shepherds and their mates, as "The happi'est innocent'st people in the World," and their first long song (*"Shepherds awake . . ."*) contrasts sharply Urania's world (the pure emotionalism of "Jolly Shepherds") to the frenzied life of the courtier (the impure emotions of the King). The themes are conventional: in the government of benign Nature, in which the Sun is true king, mankind enjoys a fruitful earth where beauty can never decay. Only in such an untroubled life is poetry possible. Yet pastoral life takes into account man's innately aggressive, competitive spirit by holding sporting matches between males for nymphs. All such activities end by nightfall when the nightingale's song *"does each Breast inspire/With loving heat and with Poetick Fire,"* so that pastoral life, love, and poetry are merged into a single integrated experience, free from monarchical contentions. Indeed, *"little showres of rain, or hail,/Which seldom do this place assail"* are the only enemies. Major distinctions between pastoral and "ordinary" life are strong in the final stanza:

> *We live aloof from Destiny,*
> *(That only quarrells with the Great)*
> *And in this Calm Retreat,*
> *(Content with Nature uncorrupted) we*
> *From splendid miseries of Courts are free;*
> *From pomp, and noise, from pride, and fear,*
> *From factions, from divisions cleer,*
> *Free from brave beggery, smiling strife,*
> *This is indeed a Life. . . .*

Yet these prelapsarian pleasures and mysteries heighten a sense of tension between Urania's life and that at court. Christian ideas of a *"Calm Retreat"* and a Golden *"Nature uncorrupted"*; the shepherds' insistence that they are not "great" people; oxymoronic references to non-pastoral (*"brave beggery," "smiling strife"*); the pastoral paradox that a shepherd's *"little Cabans stronger are,/Than Palaces"*—in these, as in other ways, the singers enjoy a political, economic, moral, social and, above all, emotional ease which civilized man, more complex and neurotic in his desires, never or rarely experiences.

The sequence shows the real, insoluble differences between court and country, and even Urania is beginning to sense the foreignness of the place so far removed from the simple greatness which she epitomizes. The whole court *senses* her glory, yet it cannot properly understand it or adjust to it. Some grow lustful, some envious, or merely appreciative, or (like Endymion) some are willing blindly to sacrifice themselves to it. Yet none can bend his "humor" to it, can surrender totally to the jolly shepherd's existence, for each is too imbued with the manners of civilized life. When this masque ends, news of Theander's conquests causes the court to exchange swiftly the pleasures of pastoral illusion for pleasures more familiar to them. They fervently sing of Mars, of animalistic violence, of bloody battles, and aggressive heroes. Their music crystallizes the deliriums of non-pastoral. In the last act, Theander, the votary of Mars (chief enemy of pastoral peace) is reunited with the embodiment of that peace, but there is an ironic, heroic justification for their impossible union. The greatly brave deserve the greatly fair. Only such types are capable of blending what for most men cannot be blended, and this is their special heroic triumph.

II *Prospero and Psyche in Operatic Garb*

Modern critics tend to agree that the Dryden-Davenant adaptation of *The Tempest* (the version on which Shadwell based his opera) constitutes perhaps the greatest esthetic crime perpetrated against Shakespeare by the Restoration.[2] We must indeed agree with Hazelton Spencer that this adaptation destroyed "the noble serenity" of the original.[3] The co-authors debased and made absurd the conditions of Prospero's magic island, particularly in their manner of creating new characters to "balance out" Shakespeare's. To match Miranda, the girl who has never seen a young man, they created her rather witless and wanton sister, Dorinda. For Sir Walter Scott, the conversations on sex of these "Two Cherubins" were mere smut, a perfect instance of the Restoration playwright's habit of catering to the perverted tastes of an audience which found comic such things as naïve girls talking (unwittingly) "the language of prostitution."[4] The adapters also provided a mate and sister for Caliban, the blobbering female monster Sycorax, Trincalo's "Queen *Blouze* the First." To Ariel too they gave a mate, Milcha, who appears but briefly in the last moments of the play; but, in Shadwell's opera, she is brought in early principally to sing duets with Ariel. What has most consternated critics, however, is the inclusion of Hippolito, "one that never saw Woman, right Heir to the Dukedom of *Mantua*," whom Prospero saved in his flight from Italy. Hippolito has been kept hidden on another part of the island, even from Miranda and Dorinda. And his existence constitutes but one of the many unlikely conditions of the action.

Yet, as these few examples show, Dryden and Davenant were aiming at comic effects quite different from Shakespeare's; they were using Prospero's fantastic world as a springboard for boldly satiric recognitions of human behavior. The Restoration *Tempest* is, in many ways, a kind of critical comment on Shakespeare's romanticism, a burlesque indeed, on "the noble serenity," for it studies the life of an "uncivilized" island from what may be called a comical Hobbist viewpoint. The Restoration adapters observe man in a raw, undeveloped society, but they modify their observations by the supernatural mysteries of Prospero's extraordinary magic. For his domain is still a highly mysterious place in the adaptation, even though its mystery is persistently exploded by a series of comic social and universal recognitions. Miranda is curious about life and sex, and she expresses herself in unwittingly obscene ways; but she still represents a very elemental aspect of girlhood. She is the innocent, chaste, innately virtuous heroine, the fine product of her father's "moral" education. Yet Dryden and Davenant cannot refrain from satirizing Prospero; his ability to educate morally proves a dismal failure when we observe his second daughter, Dorinda, who like Gartrude in *A True Widow*, reveals a deeply rooted wantonness, an innately avid sexuality. Her presence then is a comment on Miranda's purity and on Prospero's fallibility as a pedagogic guide. Shakespeare's Caliban must have suggested to the adapters a perfect study of Hobbes's portrait of "nasty, brutish" primitive man; but by adding his sister, they intensified and vulgarized the primitive horror of monstrous humanity. Sycorax is the *female* monster, a grotesque counterpart of the aggressive, amazonian lady of Restoration drama, a *reductio ad absurdum* of primordial femininity. She may fruitfully be compared to that other type of simple primitive, the fine, delicate pastoral lady, Urania of *The Royal Shepherdess.*

But it is in Hippolito that man's primordial nature is most emphatically and wittily expressed. A youth of wildly basic passions, he reacts lustily to the females, believing that his passions are intended for "all" women. His language and action are ludicrous commentaries on libertinism as it was expressed less absurdly in the rakes of Restoration comedy and, more tragically, in the feverish hedonism of Don John in Shadwell's *The Libertine*. In a humorous way, Hippolito confirms the essentially animalistic nature of man as he confirms also, before the comedy ends, man's ability to become civilized, to conform to monogamous and idealized love. Dryden and Davenant exaggerate the potential absurdities of the Shakespearean situation, even to the extent of showing that the all-powerful Prospero is as much a creature of circumstances as his subjects on the enchanted island. He may raise a tempest, entice Ferdinand to him by the hypnotic music of Ariel, terrify old enemies with horrendous "moral" antimasques of Devils, but, when his beloved Hippolito is wounded and dying after a duel with Ferdinand, Prospero sees himself also as subject to the uncertainties of the human condition. All his magic cannot compete with Death.

In Shadwell's operatic version of the Dryden-Davenant adaptation, he retained the brief lyrical passages and made a few minor excisions in the dialogue. His chief contributions are the elaborate musical settings and specific directions for a sumptuous *mise en scène*. These additions are not merely extraneous, for the adaptation suggested to him the range from absurdity to harmony; and he intensified the harmonious vision in the lavish finale as he stressed the absurd in the fantastic tempest scene which opens the opera. This scene introduces the symbolic natural and supernatural confusions of the enchanted world of Prospero—with its overture, its decorations, its perspective scenery, its *"several Spirits in horrid shapes flying down amongst the sailers, then rising and crossing in the Air,"* its spectacular image of the sinking ship, and the whole blaze of color and sound which is suddenly cut off, followed by total darkness and then by a shower of fire and thunder. In strong visual and musical terms Shadwell thus underscores *The Tempest's malentendues* and magic.

But in the grand finale, an entertainment which Prospero offers as a recompense "For the rough treatment" of the Italians, the harmonious conclusions are stated. The entertainment is a "prodigious," "amazing" ending created by "Art" which "doth much exceed all humane skill." And in it we move from the crude love-croaking of Sycorax, from the boisterous ditties of the drunken sailors, from the too-tender songs of Ariel and Milcha, from the grim pictures of Hell in the Devils' antimasque to a vast Olympian vision in which the major singers Amphitrite, Neptune, and Aeolus unfold and translate the crowning ideals of natural and supernatural order into a grand theatrical experience. Sublimity in its most majestic forms ends the confusions of the island kingdom. The splendor belongs not only to the characters of the play but also to the audience who may recognize in the operatic pageant the musical expression of a heightened, ordered, harmonious, esthetic experience.

It was Thomas Betterton, the famous actor-manager who, on his return from a visit to France, suggested, to Shadwell the possibility of doing a second opera based on the Molière-Corneille-Quinault *Psyché*. The success of the Dorset Garden production of *The Tempest* was no doubt an encouragement to Shadwell, and although he found certain weaknesses in the French play he set about to develop a musical extravaganza similar in concept to that of *The Tempest*. Shadwell thought that *Psyché* lacked what he called "Variety," was too "stiff," emotionally and structurally. In the Preface, he described his version as one in which *"the Scenes of Passion are wrought up with more Art,"* and instead of the six ballet-opera sequences which, tableau-like, formally introduce each of the five acts and conclude the play with a grand finale, he blended together musical and non-musical scenes to sustain an easier flow back and forth between them. This major change in the design illustrates well his concept of opera as a mode in which the author should sustain firmly the intricate relationship between dramatic and musical or scenic elements.

The plot of the opera, which comes from Apuleius' *The Golden Ass*, tells of the Princess Psyche, a mortal who after much mental and physical suffering, is ultimately deified. In the opening of Shadwell's opera, she expresses strong pastoral convictions of a love of nature. She wishes never to leave her simple, contemplative existence unblemished by the tumults of her father's court. She abhors the intrusions of others, of the fawning gallants and fops whom she can never love. But she finds that she cannot long remain isolated. Her beauty and virtue arouse fierce jealousies in several mortal and immortal women who thus doom her to an active life. Venus hates her partly because mankind has begun to adore her as if she were the goddess of love, partly because her son Cupid has fallen in love with her. Shadwell thus develops a heroic conflict between gods and mortals by focusing upon Cupid's determination to win his angry mother's approval of Psyche. Her elevation to Heaven is a grand tribute to love's power which can raise figuratively and actually mere mortals to immortality. And even though the context is Classical, Psyche's heroism and her deification suggest Christian ideas of redemption with the Princess as a kind of female saint or savior.

Yet, on the other hand, taking his cue perhaps from Apuleius or from Moliére's contributions to the French play, Shadwell generated in the heroic atmosphere certain non-heroic, comic elements. *Psyche* is also a tale of domestic jealousies, the mainspring of the action being a mother's frantic efforts to prevent her son from marrying. Quarrels between son and mother, mother-in-law and daughter are comically satiric, for Shadwell cannot resist the humorous implications of heroic life which he so often ridiculed in his comedies. Shadwell's dramatic range is thus as broad in this opera as in *The Tempest;* through music, spectacle, and dance he expands the theatrical range and brings within the context of myth and opera the comic as well as the heroic mood.

In the Preface to *Psyche* Shadwell spoke of *"leaving my own Province of* Comedy, *to invade their* [the heroic poets'] *Dominion of* Rhime"; his was *"but a small incursion,"* and he resolved to *"retire"* at once from the foreign territory. It was indeed this rhymed opera which Dryden attacked most vehemently in *Mac Flecknoe*; and, although an examination of Shadwell's couplets shows no mean ability to express lucidly his characters' emotions, the poetry resists the intensive analysis which can be made of Dryden's couplets in similar plays. Dryden's couplets in the rhymed heroic plays depend fully upon the elaboration of metaphor and the proliferation of complex "heroic" motives for their effect. His verse is bombastic and florid but lucid and appropriate for stage recital.

Shadwell's approach to dramatic verse is to simplify extensively the style and the ideas, to avoid excessive and elaborate "movements of the mind," though not bombast or lyricism in the dialogue. His style is lucid and it is best in the operatic scenes. In the non-operatic portions, where characters argue, rage, or woo, ideas are expressed with the minimum of metaphor. Such "poetry of statement" proves successful only when the passions being expressed are powerful enough to carry the burden of the statement, when *what* is being said (rather than the *way* it is being said) captures our attention. Such a scene as that in which Psyche and Cupid meet for the first time provides an excellent example of Shadwell's lucid, denotative expression of erotic love. It was, and rightly so, a scene of which Shadwell was especially proud.

The operatic portions are far more successful poetically. The songs of *Psyche*, like those of *The Royal Shepherdess*, crystallize and compress the larger implications of the action and theme. For example, Pan's tribute to Psyche early in the opera emphasizes the potent effects of the heroine on men and gods. Pan, like everyone else, has yielded to the *"all-commanding hand"* of *"Great Psyche, Goddess of each Field and Grove,/Whom every Prince and every God does love."* The self-imposed retreat from her father's palace is celebrated by "Flajolets, Violins, Cornets, Sackbuts, Hoa-boys" and by singers and dancers in a pastoral landscape which Psyche's presence has made *"so calm and so sweet."* Psyche's stately detachment from the world, like the Lady's in Milton's *Comus*, inspires the infernal world to tempt and to threaten her. The allegory of Ambition, Power, Plenty, and Peace (four women who want Psyche to seek worldly riches) is followed by a "dreadful Vision" of six Furies who promise to torment her for arrogantly denying a potential for evil.

The basic struggles—between good and evil, between Psyche's virtue and worldly temptations and threats of hellish torture—are hence clearly outlined in these musical portions of Act I, and the rest of the songs in the play punctuate similar crucial themes. Act V uses music to resolve the conflicts of the heroine's life, for it unfolds in a series of tableaux arrangements her mythic ascension as a goddess. In this act, which opens with a scene in Hell, Furies and Devils celebrate the Plutonic empire, their songs suggesting both the horror of the place and, at the same time, the satiric essence of their lives:

> *How little did Heav'n of its Empire take care,*
> *To let Pluto take the Rich, Witty and Fair:*
> *While it does for it self Fools and Monsters preserve,*
> *The Blind, Ugly and Poor, and the Cripple reserve.*
> *Heav'n all the worst Subjects for it self does prepare,*
> *And leaves all the best for the Prince of the Air.*

Pluto and Prosperine interrupt the preparations for torturing Psyche whom Venus has sent to the underworld. Pluto acknowledges the limits of his domain: Hell cannot keep Psyche, for *"Beauty and Innocence in Hell are free."* She belongs to the gods above, especially to the God of Love. Cupid finally convinces Venus that Psyche deserves to be his wife and so resolves the domestic melodrama of gods and mortals. Psyche rises with

Cupid to Jupiter's Palace. She emerges as the symbol of the divine love that can save mortals, just as she was saved by it. The Christian implications of her resurrection inform the imagery of the grand finale. One by one the singers (Apollo, the Elysian lovers, Mars, and Bacchus) praise the superior value of the wedding of the celestial pair. Jupiter's concluding blessing tells of the myth of salvation through love:

> For ever happy in your *Psyche* be,
> Who now is crown'd with Immortality;
> On Earth Love never is from Troubles free,
> But here 'tis one Eternal Extasie:
> 'Mongst all the Joys which Heav'n and Earth can find,
> Love's the most glorious Object of the Mind.

Such lines as these express the essence of a romantic-heroic attitude which Shadwell always regarded as a primary target for criticism not only in his comedies but in his two tragedies, *The Libertine* and *Timon of Athens*. The happy eternity which spreads before Cupid and Psyche is, indeed, a special and a rare vista in Shadwell's world.

III *Don Juan and Timon*

Claude La Rose, Sieur de Rosimond's *Le Nouveau Festin de Pierre, ou L'Athée Foudroyé,* a blank verse adaptation of Molière's *Le Festin de Pierre,* served as Shadwell's primary source for his dramatic rendering of the Don Juan legend.[5] Like Rosimond, he explored the philosophic basis of Juan's life and intensified his brutality, making him barbarous leader of a trio of iconoclasts for whom all social, natural, and religious laws (as civilization has preserved them) are irrelevant. Shadwell's John is a tragic rake, damned by an irrevocable hatred of all things good and decent. He shares with the heroes of Restoration heroic tragedy a superhuman dynamism and lawlessness, but he differs from them in that he cannot subject ultimately his ego to the dictates of an ideal lady or power. Unreformable, he can never channel his ferocious energies for the good of the civilized world.

Don John shares with the Restoration comic heroes a flippant hedonism, yet he differs from them in that his lust is evil, violent, cruel, and darkly destructive. He is animalistic, like Hippolito in *The Tempest*, but not naïvely so. And, although he resembles the prodigal Sir Humphrey of *The Woman-Captain*, he lacks the good-naturedness of that hellbent rake. This is simply to say that, while *The Libertine* derives much from contemporary comic and heroic-tragic drama, it is not a study of the comic follies or of the heroic triumphs of libertinism: it treats of iconoclasm gone mad. It sketches fiercely Hobbes's "nasty, brutish" man who, despite his courage, intelligence, and aristocratic heritage, pits his entire being against all Classical and Christian ideas of law, order, and love. Don John's career etches the darkest extreme of libertinism, and that bestiality lurking in the hearts of men bursts forth in him in a terrible passion for disorder.

The opening scene delineates the basic assumptions of John's philosophy. He and his friends, Don Lopez and Don Antonio, members of his Cult of Disorder, meet together to describe the sins they have committed during the day—like the hags reporting to the Devil in *The Lancashire Witches*. Unanimously, they re-affirm, in the hammer-like cadences of Shadwell's blank verse and prose, their credo: what other men, who are fools, call sin, *they* call pleasure. Conscience, a "fond fantastick thing," is merely cowardice and, for Antonio, "A sensless fear" that makes men "contradict/The only certain Guide, Infallible Nature." But the oracular pronouncements summing up their motivation are put forth by John:

> Nature gave us Senses, which we please:
> Nor does our Reason war against our Sense.
> By Natures order, Sense should guide our Reason,
> Since to the mind all objects Sense conveys.

The men's crimes specifically illustrate the philosophy. Lopez killed his elder brother for the family estate. Antonio seduced and impregnated his sisters. John killed his father and Don Pedro, the Governor of Seville (two embodiments of authority), plundered churches, raped and killed nuns, and committed some "thirty Murders, . . . frequent Sacrilege." All these sins inspire John to wage with greater intensity his war against human ideals which are for him absolute perversions of truth: "On, on my

Soul, and make no stop in pleasure,/They're dull insipid Fools that live by measure." These lines clearly echo the comic rakes' attitude toward convention and conventional people who pretend to virtue but who are merely afraid to express their *real* (their animalistic) emotions, who conceal hatreds and lusts beneath the masks of familial, social, political, and religious forms and attitudes. John carries further the iconoclastic vision and is remorseless as a critic of these forms and attitudes. If we consider his idea of love as mere lust of a temporary nature which seeks endlessly new objects for its pleasures in contrast to the ideation of love in the deification of Psyche, the dark side of John's life, his incapacity to rise above his senses, is seen unquestionably as a heroic deficiency.

The tragedy is developed picaresquely in a series of episodes in which John and his disciples commit crime after crime with joyous sadism. In Act I, John murders Octavio, Maria's lover; disguises himself as Octavio and seduces Maria; and then slays her brother, who has come to defend her honor. All these events occur very rapidly. Indeed, throughout the tragedy Shadwell's method of compressing time and of intensifying the atrocities suggests dramatically the incredible speed of John's destructive life. Act II shows him rejecting six wives and fiancées (one of them kills herself) and informing them that his passion was temporary. Words and bonds mean nothing to him. He changes masks at will. Only his ends matter, and the women can hardly force him to be what they want him to be.

John then orders his comic servant Jacomo to drag in from the street women whom he and his friends can seduce—in Act II, an elderly woman. His crimes of Act I have not been forgotten by Maria who, accompanied by her maid Flora, pursues him. But he murders Flora and then later Maria. He slays the hospitable Don Francisco whose daughters he attempts to seduce and whose bridegrooms he kills. In Act III he poisons the faithful Leonora who comes to help him escape from Seville. He disperses a group of happy shepherds and shepherdesses (characters who lucidly heighten distinctions between John's frenzied life and their easy pastoral joys), seducing or murdering these characters. He blasphemes at Don Pedro's grave; and in the final minutes of the play, when his father's ghost and Don Pedro's statue bid him to repent, he refuses. True to *his* ideal, without a hint of remorse, he sinks into hell clouded by fire and accompanied by devils.

The tragedy concludes, therefore, with an affirmation of divine law and order; but the dilemma which Shadwell's John posits is freighted with insoluble, ironic meanings. John's defiance of order is tragic; his nature bends him toward destruction. His own "death wish" is ultimately answered; but, within the context of the play and despite John's cruelties, we are not meant to appreciate placidly his punishment, for it does not silence the criticism he makes of law and order. We must, first of all, recognize the obvious fact of John's dissent. We must then perceive not the validity of his dissent, but the great function of law which preserves civilization and maintains man's ideals, *despite* the disillusionments of human hypocrisy, pretension, and folly. The powers that excise John play significant parts in a universe which wants to rise above the libertine vision. To rise above it, man must ascribe to the wisdom of another oracle, Christ. Ideals of love, generosity, selflessness, decency—however "artificial" they may seem—preserve whatever peace the world can offer. In a different context and with different conclusions, Shadwell reexamined these ideals in his next tragedy, *The History of Timon of Athens, the Man-Hater.*

"On the whole," Hazelton Spencer wrote, commenting on the body of seventeenth-century revisions of Shakespeare, "I am inclined to rate this adaptation [Shadwell's *Timon*] as the best, or at any rate as the least objectionable."[6] The Editor of the Arden Edition of Shakespeare's play is more critical of this first and best-known rehandling of *Timon:* "History has been less than fair to Shadwell as a dramatist . . . ; but his *Timon* certainly does him little credit. Even if he could be excused for giving Timon both a faithful mistress, Evandra, and an unfaithful one, Melissa, with the consequent triteness of plot, he can hardly be pardoned for the triteness of language, so inadequate to the tragic theme."[7] He then criticizes Shadwell's manner of having the Man-hater die on the stage but praises him for heightening the contrast between Timon and Alcibiades and the distinction between their hatred of Athens.

Shadwell's major alteration is, indeed, the creation of the two contrasting women—Evandra, the faithful cast-off mistress who commits suicide after Timon dies; and Melissa, the unfaithful woman who flatters him when he is rich but deserts him when he is poor. The elucidation of Alcibiades' roles, the second major alteration, depends fully upon Melissa's character. She turns to him after rejecting Timon and is, in turn, rejected by Alcibiades after his military defeat of the Four Hundred. These alterations affect considerably the texture of Shakespeare's play, but Shadwell's main design is similar to the original in tracing the sudden metamorphosis of a generous Athenian aristocrat into a mad, animalistic misanthrope who rages philosophically and pathetically over the horror of being human.

Timon is dedicated to the Duke of Buckingham who may have encouraged Shadwell to adapt the play, and it is notable that this play, like his only other tragedy, develops certain themes central to his comic vision. Of *The Libertine* something has already been said in this connection. In *Timon,* the parallels between the tragic prodigal and the comic prodigal are evident in Timon's failure to see how false are those friends who enjoy his lavish banquets and gifts, how much men are slaves to their senses, how different a faithful from an unfaithful woman can be. All this is knowledge which any one of Shadwell's comic heroes possesses long before the action begins. Timon's "tragedy" is that he must learn these things and yet rise above them. He resembles most the gullible spendthrift Sir Humphrey in *The Woman-Captain,* a man shattered by a belated awareness of infidelity and meanness. Evandra's presence in Shadwell's version contributes an ironic element (however obvious the irony is) which undercuts the accuracy of his excessive misanthropy. She remains true to him, but his immense disillusion blinds him to her rare virtue which transcends her promiscuity. She is forever his loyal and "virtuous" mistress.

Hazelton Spencer praised Shadwell's style in *Timon.* Unlike the Arden Editor, he saw in it "a certain rude vigor, which, while it is almost as far from Shakespeare's as anyone's, is preferable to the ineptitudes and inanities of Nahum Tate and the vandalism of D'Avenant."[8] This "rude vigor" is, in part, accomplished by reducing and compressing Shakespeare's thought and by adding new brief scenes and dialogue. As in Shadwell's rhymed plays, he tends to express "grand" themes with language as plain as possible. This tendency is more successful than in the rhymed plays, because the ideas in *Timon* are sufficiently profound to carry the burden of interest and do not require complex figurative elaboration. The blunt blank verse, moreover, contributes to our impression that Timon's world is harsh, direct, emphatic.

The proper tragic style is hinted at in the tragedy itself. Early in the action, Demetrius, Timon's honest steward, questions the fawning Poet about verse-making. The Poet insists upon generic distinctions in style, in strict Neoclassical terms. "What d'ye mean by style?" Demetrius asks, "that of good sence is all alike; . . . with apt and easie words, not one too little or too much: And this I think is good style." Astonished by Demetrius' unsophisticated grasp of poetic values, the effete Poet explains: "Heroicks must be lofty and high sounding;/No easie language in Heroick Verse"; it would be as indecorous to call a lion a lion in a heroic poem as it would be to call him an ass. A lion must, by circumlocution, become a "sounding" image, "The fierce *Numidian* Monarch of the Beasts." Demetrius denies the Poet's thesis. "Sound" is all the Poet wants; *he* himself prefers plain sense. Since Shadwell's tragic style must be described as "plain," can we conclude that he approved of Demetrius' attitude?

Clearly, the steward dislikes whatever masks reality. He is a pragmatist; and his Baconian distaste for "mere words" is intensified by the knowledge that the Poet (like all of Timon's false friends) uses words to hide his real selfishness. But clearly also the steward cannot see that feelings and truths may demand a heightened style suiting the sense and expressing figuratively those emotional and intellectual ideas which are too complex to be stated plainly. In the course of Timon's decline, *both* attitudes toward language—language as deceptive mask and as a source of candidness—are extremes which are examined and seen to be inadequate.

There are numerous instances of the use of language as deceptive mask. For example, Melissa's false expressions of devotion hide her real dislike of her bridegroom Timon in Act II: "Upon my knees I swear—/Were I the Queen of all the Universe, And

Timon were reduc'd to rags and misery,/I would not change my love to him." Although this speech is not distinctively figurative, it inaccurately reflects her mind. It stands in contradistinction to her speeches at her toilet in which she confesses to her servile maid Chloe the shallow self-love which informs her coquetry. When Timon is "reduc'd to rags and misery," she totally invalidates her vows.

On the other hand, strict truthfulness which Demetrius prefers forms, in *Timon*, another extreme sinning on the side of crassness rather than pretense. The misanthropic Apemantus states relentlessly his vision of decadent humanity in a style which recalls the virulence of old Snarl in *The Virtuoso*. In Act I he rages against all men: "What is this foolish animal man, that we/Should magnifie him so? a little warm,/And walking Earth that will be ashes soon. . . ." In Act II, he attacks the Poet:

> Thy Poetrie's insipid, none can taste it:
> Thou art a wordy foolish Scribler, who
> Writ'st nothing but high-sounding frothy stuff;
> Thou spread'st, and beat'st out thy poor little sence,
> 'Tis all leaf-gold, it has no weight in it.

This old truth-teller employs figurative language when it sharpens his meaning; in the preceding lines there are, perhaps, echoes of Donne's "gold to airy thinness beat." Apemantus' scorn is sincere enough, but like a "humor," it dominates him and prevents him from experiencing deeper or finer emotions of the kind which make life less dreadful than he insists it is.

Such emotions are expressed by Evandra. Her strained but truthful feelings of unrequited love are stated in melodramatic effusions which mirror accurately her feelings. These effusions, sustained throughout the play, reach an appropriate peak of intensity in the last scenes in the wood before she and Timon die. And in them, ultimately, Timon discovers the significance of attaining one true, selfless love—his tragic recognition in Shadwell's drama. He had his faithful love all along, but he was deflected from it by a desire to be loved by the whole world. Cut off from society with Evandra in a symbolic wood where he is closest to nature, he learns that her words are constant indices of her nature, from "The first storm of your Love [which] did shake me so,/It threw down all my leaves, my hopeful blossoms" to her final act of suicide in which she keeps her word to join Timon in death. Her last speeches are heavily melodramatic, but after Timon's demise she moves almost totally away from overt simile, becoming plainly direct in statement: "He's gone! . . . would all the world were so,/I must make haste, or I shall not o'retake/Him in his flight." For Shadwell, then, style depended upon circumstance; there was a time for ornateness as there was for simplicity, though he preferred usually the barer style.

Timon's fall from his role as the darling of Athenian society to his transmogrification as the half-mad animal clutching the gold he has drawn from the earth, leads to various recognitions. He scorns his former friends and hates the very ground of the city that betrayed him. His sharp reversal from extreme kindness to extreme ironic and virulent criticism (in Act III's mock feast and in the various rejections of the flatterers in Act V when he is rich again) shows his tragic incapacity to assume a more moderate, stoic position vis-à-vis mankind. Alcibiades, who triumphs over Athens and who (like Timon) hates the city, understands Timon's weakness; but he remains an Athenian and he resumes, after the city's betrayal, the normal business of living. Alcibiades is something of a "tragic" rake. He flaunts the law; and, as Apemantus sees him, is a proud warrior who would destroy a kingdom to gratify his self-love. Yet Alcibiades turns his personal passions and hatreds into something worthwhile. He frees Athens of its tyrants and himself from exile. In short, he triumphs publicly over those who prevent his happiness. Timon cannot move beyond his grim recognitions; he cannot accept the reality of his own and other people's failings. Like Don John, he withdraws completely under the burden of his own personality.

CHAPTER 6

The Muse That Sometimes Faltered

IN 1689, with the accession of William and Mary, Shadwell succeeded Dryden as Poet Laureate; most of the verse upon which his reputation as a non-dramatic poet rests was composed immediately before and during this appointment until his death in November, 1692. To compare Dryden's and Shadwell's laureate effusions is to confirm the universal opinion that the second is undoubtedly the inferior poet. C. V. Wedgwood's description of Shadwell's "official" poetry as "threadbare and pretentious" may be regarded as typical: "In no circumstances," Wedgwood remarks, "and with no subject, would he have been even a passable poet. (He was a lively and efficient writer of comedies; his talent was essentially earthy, colloquial, and prosaic.)"[1] This blanket rejection can be called accurate, however, only if applied to Shadwell's "official" poems, his celebrations of affairs of state. It is inaccurate if applied to other kinds of poetry where he did express his "earthy, colloquial" talent—to his songs and, above all, to his prologues and epilogues to the plays.

The brief, usually satiric prologues and epilogues constitute one of the four groups into which Shadwell's verse may be divided. The songs from the plays constitute a second group. Both groups (together with the verse-plays and the operatic portions of *The Tempest* and *Psyche*) comprise the bulk of his poetic output. These pieces may be read independent of the plays, despite the possible objection that, deprived of their context, such readings may be inadequate.[2] At any rate, they clearly prevent facile rejections of Shadwell's metrical abilities. The third group consists of two satires: his ferocious attack on Dryden (*The Medal of John Bayes*) and his translation of Juvenal's Tenth Satire, to which he prefixed a translation of a brief poem by Lucan.[3]

Some twelve, possibly fourteen poems of tribute to public figures make up the fourth and least impressive group. These occasional poems, conventional in style and imagery, range in tone from the good-natured obscenities of the doggerel "Letter to Wycherley" to the serious, torturously self-conscious celebrations of royal affairs in such pieces as *A Congratulatory Poem to the Most Illustrious Queen Mary Upon Her Arrival in England* and *On His Majesty's Conquests in Ireland*.[4] In this group may be included the poem to Pietro Reggio (who set to music Shadwell's "Arise ye subterranean winds" of *The Tempest*) and "A Song for St. Cecilia's Day, 1690."

I Prologues and Epilogues

Like many Restoration prologues and epilogues, Shadwell's thirty-six pieces in this genre explore a variety of themes in a racy style that ranks them with the best of the age.[5] His major subject is the relationship between the playwright and his audience. Their witty vitality depends largely upon the "character" of the speaker who usually addresses the audience in behalf of the playwright. The speaker's tone and attitude vary and shift, within a single poem, from grimly serious to frivolously indifferent as he cajoles, compliments, or "trepans" the audience into admiring the play. He distinguishes between the witty, true critics and the brawling "monkies" of the pit; pleads for applause by the use of an obviously false logic; blasts the audience because he anticipates its "crying down" the play. He often opens his monologue wearing the pathetic-comic mask of a harassed actor, yet invariably before he concludes, his mask shifts. He becomes the aggressor and scolds the dull audience for its pathetic-comic ignorance. The shifts are subtle, requiring careful descriptive analysis to explain them accurately.

Besides the character of the speaker and the dominant theme which bind together any single prologue or epilogue, there is generally a single image or metaphor which helps to create a witty unity in presenting the playwright-audience motive. Shadwell's favorite metaphor is of a war between artist and audience in which the playhouse is the battlefield. The artist faces his eternal enemies in box and pit, enemies who (the speaker says) can destroy the artist with mere hisses or who can permit him

The Muse That Sometimes Faltered

graciously to win the battle of one against many by their precious applause. In the Prologue to *Epsom-Wells,* written for a private performance for Charles II and the Queen at Whitehall, the speaker makes overt the usually submerged war metaphor:

> *Poets and Souldiers used to various chance,*
> *Cannot expect they should each day advance;*
> *Sometimes their Wreaths they miss, sometimes obtain;*
> *But whensoe're one luckie hit they gain,*
> *Loudly the triumphs of that day they boast,*
> *And ne're reflect on all their Battels lost. . . .*

The monarchs' interest in *Epsom-Wells* constitutes a special victory for the artist. By praising their wise approval, Shadwell (with the tongue-in-cheek humor that characterizes these pieces) praises himself. In the Prologue to *The Libertine,* the theatrical battlefield becomes a road of reconnaisance along which the wary artist-as-merchant travels with his priceless cargo of a play, and the speaker is his spy sent ahead to report what privateers, "*what bloudy Criticks were come out.*" In the Epilogue to this play, Jacomo, Don John's squire, is the speaker. At first, he peevishly attacks the enemy (even before it has had the chance to express its reactions to the drama). He rudely asks the audience to leave the theater, for to him they are as merciless as the Don in their hatred of the triumphs of civilized life, of art, and of the truth with *The Libertine* expresses. But suddenly, Jacomo, as if realizing that without an audience there can be no play, changes his tone and attitude. He recalls the audience and less belligerently offers a compromise, a peace treaty, the articles of which provide that Shadwell supply compliant actresses to keep the noisy fops busy, while the witty members of the audience may judge the play without distraction. In a sense, these "*Articles o'th' Treaty*" solve nothing; the treaty ironically points up that what is going on in the theater (the noise and the love-chasing) will never end and that the playwright can expect only the intelligent members of his audience to judge meaningfully of the play.

In the Epilogue to *The Woman-Captain,* the war theme is developed in direct relation to the comedy. Mrs. Gripe, in military costume, champions the author. As she did in the comedy, she will "correct" by brute force all fools who refuse to applaud Shadwell. Her challenge ends with a comic shift depending upon the sexual ambiguities of her threats; if there be any critic "*So careless of his Life to anger me,*" he must "*take my Glove, for I'll have Satisfaction.*" In the Prologue to *The Amorous Bigotte,* spoken by Charlotte Butler who played the termagant courtesan Levia, the war turns into a hissing contest between audience and lubricious lady. "*Against Bear-garden Hissers,*" Levia declares "*open War*":

> *Send out the fiercest Champion of your Camp:*
> *Let me the proudest of the Hissers see, . . .*
> *Soon shall the Lists your doubty Warriour quit,*
> *Taught by my single Courage to submit.*

The serio-comic notion of Shadwell being protected by such amazonian women against the snakes in the audience makes this Prologue (like many others) a kind of drama "in little," which depends heavily upon characterization and sexual *double entendres* for its total effect.

In the metaphors of the prologues and epilogues, the playhouse is often other things besides a battlefield—the setting for the victories and defeats in artistic life. As I have suggested, it may be a highway or a sea where the enemy lies in ambush. Often it is a law court, its audience the judges, the play a "crime," and the author a young woman, sometimes a wanton, being tried for her efforts to seduce the theatergoers. In Shadwell's Epilogue to Laurence Maidwell's *The Loving Enemies,* the speaker is a lawyer pleading for the poor poet who has entered the "*barren Trade*" and whose play marks his first appearance "*at this Bar.*" Perhaps with a pun upon Maidwell's name, the speaker insists that failure to applaud (a heavy sentence) would be as "*hard, as for a Girl, fresh, at sixteen,/To meet, at the first Venture, the mishap,/To lose her Maidenhead, and get a* Clap." The pun on the *one* "Clap"—as opposed to the many claps requested for Maidwell—collapses the notion of a "serious" trial, turns seriousness into insouciant levity, and sustains the humorously satiric texture of this monologue, as of others in which similar devices are used.

In several of these poems, the theater is metaphorically a

bawdy house or place of assignation; the play is a new mistress, the audience a group of keepers, the playwright the procurer. This manner of personifying the play serves occasionally as the basis for a metaphor in which the speaker introduces the traditional idea of the play as child, author as mother, audience as a committee of esthetic mid-wives, and theater as hospital. The poet is sometimes a caterer who (like the pander, the wanton, or the merchant) has something special for his audience. As caterer, he provides a nutritious meal; and the spectators, as ravenous beasts, come cannibalistically to consume it, cannibalistically because the play is that portion of his genius which he is willing for them to have. In all these roles, he regards his audience as an agent who shares in the dramatic-creative process. Yet he must often insult the audience into accepting his offering. In the Prologue to *The Virtuoso,* he contrasts the "appetizers" of rhyming plays to the nutritional main course of "humors" comedy:

> You came with such an eager appetite
> To a late Play, which gave so great delight;
> Our Poet fears, that by so rich a Treat,
> Your Palates are become too delicate.
> Yet since y'have had Rhime for a relishing Bit,
> To give a better taste to Comick Wit.

In the Epilogue to *Timon of Athens,* Shadwell talks of foolish food served by French fashion (the *"Slight kickshaw Wit o'th' Stage, French-meat at Feasts"*) which *"daily tantalize the hungry Guests"* in the banquet room of the theater. The diners need something meatier, heartier to give them health. Other figurative associations of the playwright-play-audience-theater relationship state in different ways the theatrical experience with different kinds of comic-serious meanings: the navigator-ship-storm-sea figure; the sick man-disease-physician-hospital figure, with applause as the cure; the playwright and play as quarry, the audience as hunters, the theater as forest. Shadwell's variations on the theme are numerous.

Shadwell's later prologues and epilogues, beginning with those to *The Squire of Alsatia,* explore topical themes more intensely than do his earlier ones. He keeps the idea of the theatrical war, but he subsumes new themes under it. He talks of King William's militarism, of dramatic censorship, of the crucial distinctions between England and Europe, and of his own illness in strongly serious tones which are, however, often undercut by the ironic laughter of the speaker before the poem ends. The prologues to *The Squire* and *Bury-Fair* sketch briefly the history of the English stage. The speaker laments the decline of comedy; says that Shadwell's seven-year silence hardly helped comedy survive; and finds that, with William and Mary in power, common sense and Shadwell have returned to the theater and that the stage can expect a happier future. Significant people (like Shadwell) no longer will have their art judged good because they hold the correct political views.

The Epilogue to *Bury-Fair* praises the "Brave Youths" who fight in William's wars and thanks the audience for being too cowardly to leave England; staying behind, they fill the theater and support it. This sarcastic compliment is reintroduced in the Prologue to *The Volunteers.* The speaker, for the author, agrees to pander to the bad taste of the cowardly fops who keep the theater alive; he joins their party, fawning over them as they fawn over government officials and seeking preferment at home while their heroic contemporaries die overseas.

But Shadwell's most imposing political statement in these pieces (aside from "A Lenten Prologue") occurs in the Prologue to *The Scowrers.* His range of tone and variety of subject matter are wide indeed. Playfully, he satirizes the women in the audience. They will call his comedy obscene, but they ought to know that the obscenity is produced by their minds, not by his play. He turns to the *"Witty, Fair, and Good"* women in the audience. This description he usually reserves for the heroines of his plays, and so, like a hero, he wants to please them, despite his debilitating illness. With swift-moving rhetoric and by answering rapidly his rhetorical questions, he tries persuading all the women present to be heroines—which they can be, if they like his play. His optimistic attitude toward himself and the heroines in the playhouse turns his thoughts to the question of the artist's happy position under William and Mary.

He is a happy artist (a happy man) and he abhors the "loyal" writers under Charles and James who join the malcontent critics who grumble over his deserved success. Tories may growl and cry him down *"as for his place unfit,/Since they have all the humour and the Wit,*" but he glows with pride as the new laureate. Wise William provides the proper climate for political freedom and artistic creativity; and, for Shadwell, these are inseparable. Royal approval is enough to prove his genius. The entire audience should follow suit and praise his play:

> *Till then may he that Mark of Bounty have,* ⎫
> *Which his renown'd and Royal Master gave;* ⎬
> *Who loves a Subject and contemns a Slave,* ⎭
> *Whom Heav'n in spight of Hellish plots design'd,*
> *To humble Tyrants, and exalt Mankind.*

Beginning on a note of sarcastic bitterness, moving through autobiographical allusions, expressing political attitudes, he concludes on a note of warm laureate panegyric.

Although many of these poems may not seem to be related to the plays for which they were written, there are always lines of connection, however tenuous, between poem and play. *The Scowrers* is about the education of youth, and its Epilogue treats this subject wittily and obliquely. The Epilogue to *The Amorous Bigotte* is built upon contrasts between Catholic-Spanish restrictions and Protestant-English freedom, contrasts which are indirectly treated in the play itself. The Prologue and Epilogue to *The Lancashire Witches* are closely related to the play. It will be recalled that certain politically and religiously offensive speeches were excised for the stage version, and in the Prologue, the play is metaphorically a "crippled" child for whom the speaker asks pity, if only for the sake of the actors. He blames the play's unfortunate fate on the Devil rather than on the censor (or implicitly on both together) and thus ties the poem directly to the theme of witchcraft. The Devil has bewitched modern audiences, making them admire bad and hate good plays. As a good playwright, Shadwell will draw a magic, protective circle around the true critics in the audience so that they can applaud him.

The Epilogue, cast as a dialogue between Isabella Hartfort and Father Tegue, is about the magic of women who, much like playwrights, try satisfying others with *"wondrous Art."* But we are also warned to distinguish between political and dramatic plotting, between treason and art. Tegue ought justly to be hanged for his Popish Plot, but Shadwell should not be executed for his plot in *The Witches*. Isabella ridicules the artist's eternal foes who, after the production of the play, were to hear no more, indeed, from Shadwell's dramatic Muse for almost a decade:

> If the bold Poet freely shows his Vein,
> In every place the snarling Fops complain;
> Of your gross follies, if you will not hear,
> With inoffensive Nonsense you must bear.
> You, like the Husband, never shall receive,
> Half the delight the sportful Wife can give
> A Poet dares not whip this Foolish Age,
> You cannot bear the Physick of the Stage.

The seriousness of this indictment of a society which censored the artist is typically, in these lines, blended with the playful image of the artist as "wife" and doctor.

II *Songs from the Plays*

As in Shakespeare, Jonson, or Dryden, the songs in Shadwell's plays may be studied independent of their context, although indeed, like the prologues and epilogues, the dramatic settings figure significantly in the fullest understanding of their meanings. In the operatic plays, music and song are, of course, essential to the fundamental design; in others, music and song are incidental. The songs deal primarily with three subjects: love, drinking, and hunting or war. Briefly and musically, they restate ideas which are being dramatically expressed in action and characterization, and they reinforce our understanding of both.

Their dramatic meaning depends upon the character who sings them and upon the exact contextural point in the play when they are sung. The songs function in various ways. They may reveal character. They may join together threads of the plot, punctuate themes, or foreshadow denouements. They may heighten contrasts between characters who sometimes "pit" their songs against each other. They provide "entertainments in little," translating musically comic motives within the larger, broader design of the action.

The question of reading the songs in or out of context can be clearly illustrated by one of the many drinking songs, "A CATCH in four parts":

> *Come lay by your cares, and hang up your sorrow,*
> *Drink on, he's a Sot that e're thinks on to morrow;*
> *Good store of good Claret supplies every thing,*
> *And the man that is drunk, is as great as a King.*
> *Let none at misfortunes, or losses repine,*
> *But take a full Dose of the juice of the Vine;*
> *Diseases and troubles are ne're to be found,*
> *But in the damn'd place, where the Glass goes not round.*

The *carpe diem* theme, the celebration of the curative function of Bacchus, the hint of a tavern setting in the final lines, the suggestion of an effort to convince someone to enjoy the pleasures of the tavern—all these are aspects available without a knowledge of context. The context, however, illuminates complexly the poem's meaning. This song is from Act III of *The Miser*. It is sung by the gamblers and prostitutes who are trying to establish a feeling of good-fellowship in Tim Squeeze, the dupe they wish to fleece. Fraternal themes are thus modified by comic-sinister motives, sinister insofar as poor Tim is concerned. Yet the song is also "good-natured" for it expresses accurately the sort of freedom which the commercially minded Tim is experiencing for the first time. Among "friends," he can forget the harsh world where diseases, troubles, misfortunes, and losses abound. The tavern is a curative structure, a hospital, or a heaven apart from that *"damn'd place,"* the unblessed world outside. Yet the truth is that the tavern has its own kinds of diseases, troubles, misfortunes, and losses—as yet unknown to Tim. He pays dearly for the short-lived illusion of companionship and kingship into which the Claret flatters him.

The drinking glass, symbolic of fraternity, is also a kind of looking glass. In it our real selves, no longer disguised by sobriety, are revealed. The looking glass suggests two meanings pertinent to *The Miser*: first, Tim's folly is clearly visible, but the fleecers, because they are not as drunk as he, manage to conceal rather than reveal their true characters. They enjoy conviviality, but they are business people at work on a fool.

Secondly, we see the basic difference between the underworld and Mr. Goldingham's world. Businessman's woes may be cured by nature's vine magically fermented into Claret; deception in the tavern brings at least passing pleasure. But in Goldingham's saturnine world there are no escapes (no "mirrors" or brief illusions) from crass reality.

The concluding couplet foreshadows the end of the comedy. Tim repeats the couplet later, as if recalling past joys, as if reminding us that it was at the height of these joys that he fell into fresh sorrow as the husband of a cast-off mistress. Theodore and Bellamour, in contrast, "cure" the diseases afflicted upon them by Goldingham's greed, without the doubtful assistance of wine; they escape from the imprisonment of the "*damn'd*" house of the miser into a sober life with the girls they love. Many of Shadwell's songs stress similar complexities of dramatic conflict, action, and meaning.

Most often, however, and with less complexity, the songs freeze lyrically the salient "humor" of the characters who sing them. Oldwit in *Bury-Fair* is a kind man who claims to have had Jonson, Fletcher, and Cleveland as companions; his idea of wit is to pull chairs out from under supercilious fops. He recurrently employs limerick as a blunt instrument for criticism. His insistense on candidness in a pretentious age is expressed, for instance, in the crude lines addressed to his step-daughter, Mrs. Fantast, a blatant *précieuse:* "She makes wry Mouths, and chews every word,/Like an old Sow, that simpereth with a new T—." Shadwell's use of lyric in Oldwit's case differs from his usual approach. Typically, characters are not cognizant of the ironic ways in which their songs pinpoint their flaws. Oldwit knows he is crude; he boasts of his scatological epithets "on men and beasts."

But someone like Drybob, in *The Humorists,* is blind to the self-denigration of his lyrical outbursts. He presents the heroine with a French dog and a "witty" poem in which the dog is the "speaker." He identifies with it as "*your most humble Servant and Dog*," reaching a climax in the chorus, "*With a Bow, Wow, Wow.*" Similarly, in *A True Widow,* Young Maggot compares himself to a "happy flea." His uncle, who is violently opposed to poetasting, uses the song as proof of Maggot's idiocy, but not for the right reasons. For the uncle, all poetry, good or bad, is a waste of time. Hence, while the song links the singer and the insect, it also throws light on the characters of those who listen to and comment on it.

Maggot's pastoral song, sung early in the play, is part of an informal contest between him and sportsman Prig. The better singer is presumably the better lover. The physically ugly Maggot couches facile emotions in the conventional language of lamenting shepherds, but he cannot sustain even this idyllic mood for in the final couplet he deflates everything by a clumsy shift of tone and meaning: *"My love by scorn can not be tamed,/ But I the rather would be at her."* Prig, the child-man, does no better. He is proud of his masculine boldness; and, although he does not sin on the side of cold superficiality as Maggot does, he reveals his incapacity to experience any valid emotions toward the object of his passion. His fourteen-line lyric tells the tale of a pretty maiden whom he encountered *"One Night walking in a Wood."* A man of action, he decided to seduce her immediately:

> *Quoth I, my pretty Buxom Lass,*
> *From me this time thou shalt not pass.*
> > *In any Case;*
> *For the sake of thy Face!*
> *I'll lay thee on the Grass.*

The song, giving no indication that Prig accomplished his design, points to his fruitless efforts to win Mrs. Cheatly with his plain, crude lust. The nursery-like refrains of this song (*"With a hey Boys, ding, ding, ding"*) and of his tavern song in Act II (*"Twivee, twivee, ho"*) show us a man incapable of rising above the elementary low pleasures of drinking and hunting. The contrasts between Maggot and Prig restate and emphasize what their dialogue and action make clear. In other plays, songs suggest rather intricate relationships between characters, relationships not fully expressed in the non-lyrical parts of the play. This use of song to enlarge the dramatic meaning is most evident in the plays which make ample use of lyric or masque.

Three such complex songs occur in *The Libertine*. When John woos Maria (whom he is "resolv'd to enjoy" largely because Don Octavio "likes her"), he brings musicians to sing of the sexual appetites of the *"faithful young vigorous Lover,"* erotically picturing the male as "hovering" bird and the female as the house into which the wooer demands entry. Erotic ambiguities are suggested by the words *Heart* and *faithful* which have unconventional meanings for John:

> *The* [true] *Heart that was once a Monarch in's Breast,*
> *Is now your poor Captive, and can have no rest;*
>   *'Twill never give over,*
>   *But about your sweet bosom will hover.*
>   *Dear Miss, let it in,*
>   *By Heav'n 'tis no sin:*
> *Here's a faithful young vigorous vigorous Lover.*

Then Don Octavio appears; to John, he is a mere "Serenading Coxcomb" who will sing "some damn'd Song or other, a *Chloris*, or a *Phillis* at least." Indeed, Octavio's pastoral-Platonic praise of Maria as a sun, a deity, an angel, a bright miracle, and a superhuman figure whose *"One charming Look"* can *"subdue Mankind,"* epitomizes for John the false spiritualization of the female human animal. It is against such spiritualization that he conducts his crusade, in this scene in the form of a song competition between himself and Octavio. Octavio's words conceal, in part, his sexual drives; for, like John, he intends to seduce Maria; thus something of a deep irony informs his efforts to translate lust into Platonic ideation that he might really believe in. John's tragedy is that he cannot conceive of ideal love emerging from animal instincts. Soon after the second song, the "barbarous Villain" John literally silences forever the singer of traditional, romantic illusion.

Maria may *"subdue Mankind"* in Octavio's eyes, but she cannot subdue John who seduces her (as he seduces many women) by lies, by force, and by song. When, in Act II, six of his wives and lovers claim him, he responds in a sarcastic lyric, "my *Epithalamium*," a credo of lust and a tribute to *"Wise Nature"* who teaches man the realities of *"Bless'd freedom."* The impact of the song on the women is great; they become martyrs to the illusion of faithfulness which John creates for them. Their suffering is revenged in Act V when, true to his iconoclasm, John is unmoved by the "Song of Devils" who promise, in musical pictures, *"an eternal dreadful Doom."*

Shadwell often uses song to throw into relief divergent attitudes between characters who react differently to song. In *The*

Squire of Alsatia, the army deserter Hackwell hopes to impress his fellow-criminals with his bravery, yet his song, "a very pretty magnanimous military business upon the Victory in *Hungary,*" convinces no one (save the dupe Tim Belfond) of his pretensions. Hackwell had no part in the Duke of Lorraine's triumph over the Turks, so that the Duke's real courage is finely juxtaposed to Hackwell's real cowardice. A similar ironic distinction between singer and song has already been noted in the Clodpate-Jilt scene in *Epsom-Wells,* when the Sussex fool is angered because the musician who mocks city life is, in fact, a city lover.

In *The Amorous Bigotte,* music is used in much the same way to suggest the importance of differentiating between art and nature, the song and the singer. The old soldier Don Bernardo woos the heroine Elvira by calling musicians to serenade her. They sing of the difference between passion in old and young men. The *"Fire of Love in youthful blood"* is short-lived, but in old men the steady power of love, having *"crept into aged Veins,"* is *"Like fire in logs"* which *"glows, and warms 'em long,/And though the flame be not so great,/Yet is the heat as strong."* The musicians touch the wise Elvira; she is moved by their pictures of the aged wooer. Not so the Don. He hates their theme, dismisses them, calls forth a drummer, and tortures Elvira with what he believes is music more appropriate for a military lover—the noises of a war song with its *"thump, thump,"* its *"a dub, dub a dub,"* ending in a *"Tara, tan, tan-tara, ra./This is the Soldiers Trade."* Elvira shrinks from the noise, but her sarcastic " 'Tis admirable" convinces the Don that she *is* impressed. He cannot understand how the esthetic interpretation of reality (of the fact that he is old) helped him more than his blustering pretensions to youthful vigor in his courtship of Elvira. The differences between his reactions and hers describe the impasse existing between the pair.

Most of Shadwell's songs have a pastoral setting, and the "distance" between their atmosphere and the comic world where love is often a bald pursuit of beast after beast, becomes vast indeed. In Act II of *Epsom-Wells,* the would-be adulterer Woodly teaches Carolina a new song (*"How pleasant is mutual Love that is true"*) in which pastoral elements are erotically transmuted by ambiguity and *double entendre.* The song also expresses Woodly's strong anti-matrimonial masculine position so that there is comic irony in the fact that Carolina sings it. It permits her to declare a bold libertinism without losing her feminine modesty; for, like many of Shadwell's heroines, she is skeptical about marriage. A similar effect occurs in the song that Miranda asks her maid to sing to the heroes in *The Virtuoso*. The song sardonically rejects the love game, "*a Foolish Toy*," and celebrates freedom. Like Carolina, Miranda uses song to express frankly her thoughts; but it should be remembered that Shadwellian ladies often deride love and marriage in order to stimulate their pursuers' curiosity in them as hard-to-win women.

In *The Woman-Captain*, Shadwell makes greater use of songs and snatches than in any other of his comedies. These pieces are associated with two figures, the generous Sir Humphrey Scattergood and the cowardly fool Swash. Sir Humphrey celebrates his birthday, the first day of what he plans will be a wild lifetime, with three elaborate effusions expressing key aspects of his epicureanism. The first song, "*Love thee till there shall be an end of matter*," tells of his undying love for Phillis, his prostitute; and it is freighted with libertine subterfuge. He knows that libertines can never "love eternally" for inconstancy is their hallmark. The second song (sung in the presence of greedy Gripe who prefers the "jingling" music of moneybags) celebrates the senses, the philosophical-naturalistic basis of prodigality in ways which recall Don John's songs. Its final verses, with their *carpe diem* declarations which ask men to "*Fill up the little Life that's lent*," point ironically to the end of his birthday celebrations when he loses all his money and freedom. His last lyric, "*A Drinking SONG*," Baudelairean in its languid visions of enchantment and escape, celebrates alcoholic illusion and the "*soveraign Balsom*," the "*kind purple flood*" which obliterates what is ugly in life.

Each of the three songs of this essentially intelligent and sensitive young man sharpens the great distance between his openhearted naïveté and the dissembling nature of his prostitute and of the summer friends who abandon him after his downfall. In contrast, Sir Christopher Swash's songs are crass, unintelligent, and insensitive; but their ideas are based on a philosophy similar to Sir Humphrey's.[6] Swash, a bully who enjoys breaking windows and creating havoc, states in low fashion what the prodigal says in an intricate, highly figurative way. Swash scorns Sir

Humphrey's drinking song; it cannot "make a man merry." He answers it with one of his several drinking songs:

> *Be she black, or be she brown,*
> *She's the best in all the Town,*
> *So she keep her Belly down,*
> *Down, down, down down. . . .*

Swash cannot conceive of wine's enchantments, yet his crudity serves as a kind of vulgar wisdom or protection. Although he is exposed as a coward, he experiences no fall similar to Sir Humphrey's. We might even say that his downfall has already occurred, that he is "low" enough when the comedy begins. But Sir Humphrey's finer character clearly makes him the dupe to his own "humor." These meanings are perfectly expressed in the lyrical sections of the play.

III   *Satire and Official Verse*

Aside from Shadwell's "scholarly" translation of Juvenal,[7] only one non-dramatic satire can with any degree of certainty be attributed to him, *The Medal of John Bayes*. Written in answer to Dryden's *The Medal*, it has as its target Dryden, the Bayes of the satiric burlesque *The Rehearsal;* and in certain organizational and thematic ways it follows Dryden's manner of distinguishing between the villains and the virtuous people in *Absalom and Achitophel, Part One*. Although Shadwell's satire does not tell a continuous story, it creates a set of bad versus good people—on the one hand, the archetypal villain Bayes; on the other, the noble persons whom he has betrayed, the Duke and Duchess of Monmouth, Shaftesbury, Charles II, and the people of England. But Shadwell's vituperative Juvenalian style makes so absolute his moral bias that his satire lacks the fine, ironic shades of qualification and value which distinguish the best English satires. Except from time to time, there is little subtlety in this poem of blame (as there is little subtlety in his poems of praise to William and Mary). Dryden is all bad; Shaftsbury, all good.

The poem expresses, however, other kinds of ironic awareness. In the opening couplets, Shadwell dons the Juvenalian mask and stresses differences between his wise rage and the blind one of merely crabbed, morose persons whose "humor" it is to satirize human sin. (We think of his comic characters, Stanford, Snarl, or Clodpate.) The speaker can no longer remain silent when the villain-fool Bayes is determined to destroy all that Englishmen hold good:

> How long shall I endure, without reply,
> To hear this *Bayes*, this Hackney-rayler lie? . . .
> Whilst with foul Words and Names which he lets flie,
> He quite defiles the *Satyr's* Dignity.
> For Libel and true *Satyr* different be. . . .

The personae thus prepares us for a considered definition of "true satire"—not satire of specific persons (Bayes's treacherous method), but of "the Vices of the Times," the kind of general satire which the Restoration admired. In this Shadwell echoes his Epilogue to *The Humorists* where he says of Jonson that he *"onely lash'd the Errors of the Times,/And ne'r expos'd the Persons, but the Crimes."* Yet despite the Jonsonian model, contemporary taste, and his own protestations, the speaker perversely indulges in a "foul" tirade against the "Heroick Clown" whom wise men must (and can so easily) silence. It is part of Shadwell's design, then, to do precisely what true satire should not do and what Bayes always does, attack the *person*. But he attacks the crimes as well.

The series of attacks on "this *Cherry-cheek'd Dunce* of Fifty three" take up the early part of the poem, and they incorporate many of the typical criticisms of Dryden made in the numerous satires written after *Absalom*. Shadwell is also thinking of Dryden as a "humors" character, and Dryden's "humor" of being dull gives firm unity to the portrait. Dryden himself spoke of his saturnine disposition, which the speaker calls "crabbedness," and only this "humor" can explain Bayes fully. Bayes insults crudely not only others, but also himself, thinking his lewdness is the height of wit:

> He boasts of Vice (which he did ne'r commit)
> Calls himself *Whoremaster* and *Sodomite;*
> Commends *Reeve's* Arse, and says she Buggers well,
> And silly Lyes of vitious pranks does tell.

Like Juvenal, the speaker is obscene, not because he relishes obscenity—indeed, he abhors it—but because he is an impartial "journalist" reporting facts. In Bayes's mouth the speaker puts vulgarity, so that the libelous texture of the satire is sustained even while the speaker remains a moralistic observer.

Part of Bayes's portrait is biographical. The stages of growth of his saturnine madness form a lucid structural pattern which traces from past to present a lifetime devoted to stupidity and malice, a lifetime culminating in his relationships with the good people of the poem. Although in his comedies, Shadwell usually abstains from offering moral-ethical standards by which the audience can judge the characters' actions, in *The Medal of John Bayes* he makes explicit such standards in the complimentary portraits of the good people and in his consideration of Charles II's associations with Bayes. Actually, most of the poem is about the good and about the way in which the villain gains their favor. He fashioned early his "humor," revealing it first at Cambridge when he "traduc'd" a nobleman who rebuked him only as he can be rebuked, "on the head." Among bad men, he learned new methods of malice:

> The next step of Advancement you began,
> Was being Clerk to *Nolls* Lord *Chamberlain,*
> A Sequestrator and Committee-man.
> There all your wholesome Morals you suckt in,
> And got your Gentile Gayety and Meen.
> Your Loyalty you learn'd in *Cromwels* Court. . . .

After Cromwell, the arch-rebel was ready to infect with venom the modern heroes of Restoration England. To those who showed him kindness (such as Sir Robert Howard or the Duchess of Monmouth, "Sweet *Annabel,* the good, great, witty, fair"), he gave back scandal. With the references to Monmouth's wife, the speaker moves from satiric to panegyric portraiture, providing us with a gallery of Bayes's victims, and after these to Bayes's falsification of facts concerning the Popish Plot. Even in his panegyrics, the speaker indulges in ironic qualification. The good were duped by an obvious villain; their innocence was no protection against him. Yet their innocence is their chief virtue. The satirist's task, then, is to inform and to warn even as he praises, as in his remarks on Charles: "He's *King* of all, and would have all their Hearts, . . ./He at the Peoples Head, may great appear,/As th' *Edward's, Henry's,* and *Eliza* were."

The speaker then defends the Exclusionists by insisting on *"our Legal Monarchy";* his comments reflect the Whig belief that Charles was weakening the nation when Louis and France, England's great foes, were growing stronger. At the end of the poem, the speaker returns briefly to "Mercenary *Bayes"*: the serpent has convinced no one aware of political realities that the Whigs are traitors. This conclusion is the subtlest of his criticisms of Charles who had, indeed, been so convinced. The final couplets resume the intense disapproval of the early part of the poem: "Pied thing! half Wit! half Fool!" Bayes is not a whole man. He is an unhealthy creature whose partial wit makes him witless and through whose "humor" we can predict all of his future action—a melange of knavery, cowardice, and base servility.

The Whiggish defense of a strong Parliamentary power and the idea of a social contract between crown and people in *The Medal of John Bayes* were expressed, less overtly, in the earliest of his dedications to noblemen and important officers of state. His interest in Shaftesbury's cause; his distrust of France; and, finally, Dryden's vindictive satires against him intensified his Protestant animosity toward James II and Catholicism, although his loyalty to Charles was unquestionable. This "True-Blue-Protestant Poet," as he was dubbed in the subtitle to *Mac Flecknoe,* could hardly remain politically neutral when a monarchial system had the power to silence him as a comic dramatist. With many of his contemporaries, Shadwell shared the view that Charles's Restoration had not, after all, created the ideal setting for men of artistic talent. His personal difficulties in the 1680's he must have considered an immediate example of the Stuarts' failure.

It was natural, therefore, that, with William's arrival in England in 1688, Shadwell should be among the first to publish openly his approval of the Glorious Revolution. *A Congratulatory Poem* is the first of some seven to nine poems in which he attempted to define his concept of the ideal ruler.[8] Using contemporary events against which to express dramatically the concept, he saw William as England's perfect hero and Mary as its perfect heroine. Each poem sketches a different aspect of their heroism. Each reveals Shadwell's shrewd awareness of England's mixed feelings, its fears and its expectations, concerning the new monarch from Holland.

Three major ideas in the idealized portraits bind together the official poems. First, William is characterized as a *deliverer*. Like Moses, his concern is to maintain religious-political unity and law. He is anxious to return to England its ancient ideals of equality and of sustaining a secure emotional bond between the monarch and the people. His is the true Restoration (by implication, the Restoration of Charles was a false start), and his policy goes back to the glorious reign of Elizabeth. Second, he is a *conqueror,* a war hero. In the military poems, Shadwell's main purpose is to show that William's wars in Europe (and, of course, in Ireland) were waged to protect Englishmen from the encroaching power of France and Papal Rome. Louis is the notorious villain in William's life. In the *Ode on the Anniversary of the King's Birth* (1690), Shadwell leads the chorus of patriotic voices in a song which emerges ultimately as a national anthem: "*On this glad Day let every Voice/And Instrument, Proclaim our Joys,/And let all* Europe join *in the Triumphant noise. . . .*" The international motive is pronounced in his later laureate pieces, and it is closely related to the third major idea in the portrait of William, his role as a *universal hero,* the "great example" and prototype of the epic leader—warrior, defender of law, "teacher of manners."

Mary is the female counterpart in each of the three heroic aspects. To William's role as Moses, she is a Noah whose relationship to the people stems back farther than William's. In the poem celebrating her arrival in England her ship is the Ark which survived the destructions of England's "bloody beast," her father James II. Through her Stuart line, in her marriage to a foreigner, she "brings *Olive*" and propels the "*bless'd . . . Invasion*" of Orange. To William's role as warrior, she plays the domestic heroine at home, maintaining excellently her household, her country. Naturally, she laments the absence of her "genius," but she sets also an example for all woman and is thus the prototype of perfect wife and queen, the ideal female half of a *"matchless Pair."* Like the heroines of Shadwell's plays, she is wise, fair, and good. And indeed, in the posthumously produced *The Volunteers,* the hero Hackwell, a colonel in William's army, specifically reminds the heroine Eugenia that she must imitate Mary's manner. Eugenia refuses to marry Hackwell because she fears he may die in battle; like Mary, she must learn patience, hope, sacrifice, and heroism.

Shadwell's emphatic, often "strained" effort to heighten the figures of William and Mary should not suggest that he was unaware as laureate of the difficulties created by the Glorious Revolution and particularly by the crowning of a "foreigner" who "invaded" England. William was the Protestant hero who, for many years, hoped to obtain the English crown so that, with England firmly behind him, he might successfully carry on his principal passion, his European crusades.

But was the Prince of Orange aware of the English heritage, as persons like Shadwell understood it? Did he know how concerned the nation was with domestic rather than with foreign issues and that the Irish Parliament's declaration of war against the crown in 1691 mattered more than the defeat of Louis in Flanders? Shadwell recognized the importance of such matters and, concerning the state poems as a group, he apparently considered himself as an apologist for William. Many of these poems achieve a special depth, apart from their ideating function, when we realize that, while he praises William, he also explains to William what it is the nation expects from him as its monarch. In one of his last tributes, *Votum Perenne, A Poem to the King on New-Years-Day,* Shadwell sustains the idealizing patterns, speaking for a nation that hoped for greatness in its monarch:

> No *Nation* is like ours securely Blest,
> While all the *World* is Plagu'd, we are at Rest.
> This more than *Goshen* is, the *Power Divine*
> Has made Two *Suns* in our *Horizon* shine:
> A *Prince* who bravely can abroad *orecome,*
> While his Fair *Queen* can wisely *Reign* at Home.

But he does not fail also to express his wishes for the coming year that wars cease utterly: his Muse

> ... in a *Vision* whisper'd to my Ear,
> That a more *Wondrous Scene* would yet appear,
> That my *Great Master* was by *Fate* design'd
> To *Quiet* the *Disturber* of *Mankind*. . . .
> *You Sir,* shall make those *dire Convulsions* cease
> And give the *Shaken World* a *firm* and *glorious Peace.*

Shadwell's state poems fix practical matters in perspective even as they express panegyric effusions in a manner which suggests that William's significance is quite beyond English suspicion.

CHAPTER 7

After the Period of Silence

THE two comedies which brought to an end Shadwell's period of silence, *The Squire of Alsatia* and *Bury-Fair*, are generally considered his masterpieces. They reveal his prolific comic vision, the vivid and variegated panorama of satiric existence, the dramatic picture of what he saw as mankind's perpetual folly and its rare triumphs in an age and in a world dominated by "humors."[1] Both plays remind us of his previous comedies, and his habit of returning time and again to certain standard themes, types, and situations may inaccurately suggest that he lacked "originality." As pointed out elsewhere, however, recurrent elements indicate his awareness, as a Neoclassicist, that there were themes, techniques, and characters so fundamental to the idea of comedy as he saw it that it was his task to utilize them, as a poet utilizes old myth, in each new comedy. Searching for and employing the universal elements of the mode, he refashioned his core material, qualified his concept of "humors" comedy, and re-expressed the *idea* in fresh plot formations, situations, and themes.

We may consider, for example, *Bury-Fair* in relation to *Epsom-Wells* and *The Lancashire Witches*. In each, a suburban setting expresses variations on traditional contrasts between primitive and civilized life. *Epsom* is about people on a holiday from civilization, freely enjoying themselves at a spa where nature offers them its health-giving waters. The *Witches* studies varieties of primitivism—the Adamic life of a squire's paradise, demoniac witchcraft, and comic-romantic witchcraft of charming girls who rouse the primitive passions of two city men. In *Bury-Fair*, the setting and the Fair are symbolic centers of action, and the country-city contrast is very differently expressed. The Fair is a place of ritual, a social market place where, annually, country and city people join together to buy and sell commodities—rare silks and gingerbread as well as their personalities, their ideals, their follies. At the Fair, each person declares in public view his values. Each raffles for what he calls the "goods" of the world—the human heart or silverplate, whichever he thinks will bring him happiness. Society is commerce; the Fair, a site for social action. Bad marriages, foolish and clever ladies, reforming rakes—all these we have seen before in the comedies, but not in the special foci of the Fair and of Bury St. Edmunds.

There is familiar material in *The Squire* also: good and foolish guardians in conflict; clods duped by city scoundrels; two rakes who play elaborate love games; two clever girls imprisoned by a greedy Puritan guardian and anxious to wed the men who can liberate them; a tempestuous lady disguised as a man who hopes vainly to triumph in a man's world; innumerable misunderstandings, recognitions, deceptions, punishments, and rewards. Shadwell's favorite targets of satire—education, religion, courtship, wedlock, rural dullness, and citified villainy—reappear. *The Squire* is Shadwell's most "populated" play. It is complicated by many layers of ironic contrast and comparison, and yet its strong, lucid central plot is sustained. With the skill of an excellent puppeteer, Shadwell manipulates his host of creatures without hopelessly entangling the strings. In part, his success depends upon the fact that the characters and situations are familiar, that they are instantaneously recognizable. And our pleasure stems from Shadwell's ability to re-express them with a freshness which reveals how much they were for him the inexhaustible sources of the comic mode.

I *Educating the Rake*

Shadwell's faith in the inexhaustibility of the comic mode is suggested in his source for *The Squire*, Terence's *The Brothers*.[2] Like most Restoration adaptations of Classical works, *The Squire* reconsiders the concerns of the ancient world and makes implicit the Neoclassical belief that there are universal truths about man. Such a blurring of temporal-geographical differences is also, however, counterbalanced by clear-cut *distinctions* between ancient and modern man. In many ways, Terence's second-century Romans and Shadwell's seventeenth-century Englishmen are alike, but in many ways they are startlingly different.

Both authors share a traditional, Classical concern with the problem of education and with the relationship between teacher and youthful student, with the kind of ideological heritage that is passed on from generation to generation, and with the continuity between generations. For both writers, society is in a state of constant upheaval and renewal. Its "new" people must *learn* to face an unknown future. Sometimes the teacher shows the student how to cope maturely with life's outrageous fortunes; sometimes, by wrongly educating him, he cripples the student's personality and makes him incapable of adjusting to life. On these general points, Shadwell and Terence agree; in the kinds of experience and the ultimate significance of education they differ.

In *The Brothers,* Terence tells of two aged Athenian brothers, the good-natured Micio and the crabbed Demea who has two sons. He raised one of them, the younger Ctesipho; the other, the elder Aeschinus, he permitted Micio to raise. Aeschinus' reputation as an incorrigible Athenian rake has enraged Demea who blames his son's degeneration on Micio's liberalism. But unknown to Demea, Ctesipho has run away from their country home to Athens where, tasting freedom for the first time, he goes wild, kidnaps a cittern-player from her master, and seduces her. Aeschinus, more familiar with the dangers of city living, protects his naïve brother. He has himself seduced a young girl, the good Pamphila who, during the action, is realistically heard offstage giving birth to his child. The usual comedy of errors ensues because of Demea's failure to see that his restrictive education proved useless, that his model son is as bad as Micio's ward. When Aeschinus keeps his vows and marries Pamphila, however, he proves his worth to the embittered father, and so ultimately Terence shows that easy-going educational methods are better than harsh ones, for youths must inevitably and normally sow their wild oats. Yet Terence's conclusion is subtly ironic, for the positions of Micio and Demea are comically exaggerated, and the youths are unusually lusty. A more moderate pair of pedagogic theories and young brothers would have allowed for a more sensible and serious answer to the problem of education. But the play is a comedy. These exaggerations are part of its mode.

The Squire follows *The Brothers* in its basic design by opposing two sets of brothers and two extreme theories. Long before the play begins, Sir William Belfond (Demea) retired from his rake's life in London to live in the country with his wife. After her death, he reared his elder son and heir, Timothy, in a grimly old-fashioned manner; but he sent his second son, Ned, to his brother Sir Edward Belfond, who like Micio never married. Sir Edward, something of a rake in his youth, stayed in London and amassed an independent fortune as a gentleman-businessman. He is Shadwell's embodiment of the ideal merchant, an honor both to the commercial world and to the aristocracy into which he purchased admission. He stands in utter contrast to Shadwell's earlier caricatures of businessmen (Goldingham, Gripe, and Maggot); and he points, however faintly, to eighteenth-century ideations of his type in such figures as Cumberland's Mr. Stockwell. His educational attitudes illustrate his intelligence and gentility. Like Micio, he appreciates youth's zest for freedom. But his liberalism is far more elaborately detailed and psychologically profound than Micio's.

In a series of conversations between William and Edward, the opposing theories not only serve the purposes of dramatic exposition, but punctuate and bind together the complex structural network of the comedy. In Act I, their "humors" (upon which depend their theories) are described. An excessively emotional and sour disposition is the true source of William's illiberalism. He whipped and scolded Tim, bombarding him with his moralism. He turned Tim into an oaf, and their relationship into a tyrant-slave association, the kind of relationship which Shadwell associated with the reign of the Stuarts.[3] To William, education is not ignoble. It leads to truth and morality; but these must always be practical, lucrative. The pupil must learn to answer affirmatively life's burning question: "Does he get a Shilling" by his education? Morality means frugality; immorality means prodigality—or whatever will "lose a Shilling."

Sir Edward's personality encouraged him to give Ned love, friendship, and freedom. In their second meeting in Act II, the educators provide some details of their programs. William's is purely vocational; the student must learn how to run an estate successfully. Edward's program is more painstaking, although its ends are also practical. The student must learn how to lead a worthy life, a life that is worth living. Like Ned, he should be sent to the best schools—Westminster, the University, the Temple—to absorb the timeless wisdom of the past. Afterward, he should broaden his perspectives on a grand tour to study modern culture. Like Ned, he should participate in war in order to experience actively the struggle for existence. These steps should make Ned "a Compleat Gentleman, fit to serve his Country in any Capacity." William vociferously scorns the method. Kindness and liberality have made Ned a notorious rowdy who wastes his life away.

The main action of *The Squire* is to test the value of the theories, to prove that Edward is right and William is wrong. The proof lies in the characters and careers of Tim and Ned and in the dramatic revelation of their way of coping with the problems which life throws in their paths. From the moment the comedy begins, when we find Tim in the process of being fleeced by the criminals of Alsatia, it is obvious that William's methods have hopelessly failed. Tim cannot discriminate between friend and foe, and he is well on the road to financial ruin. But it is far less clear that Edward's methods have succeeded, for although we admire Ned's suaveness, we see that his life is hardly making him a worthy patriot. Ultimately, Ned reforms and proves the value of Edward's theory. As in Terence, the worldly son saves his naïve brother from social and financial disaster.

But Shadwell fills in Terence's plot—too thin for Restoration tastes—with a profusion of characters and incidents. First, Ned saves not only Tim and himself, but several other people. He acts as an agent of English justice by destroying the Alsatian gang which has been trying to fleece Tim. Secondly, there are not two but several types of education expressed in the various relationships between older and younger characters. Thirdly, Tim becomes a full-fledged rake at the end of the play, enjoying ironically a belated "naturalism"; unlike Ctesipho, he remains a bachelor, swearing to his savior Ned, to have "my swing at Whoring and Drinking, as you had. . . ." Fourth, the irresistible Ned snares not one but three females in his amorous net. Like Aeschinus, he marries; but he does not marry his old mistress or the young girl he seduced. Finally, the two worlds of *The Brothers* (the riotous rakehell's world and the somber world of older people) are more sharply delineated in *The Squire*.

The first of these worlds is Alsatia. Alsatia was once a religious sanctuary which, by ancient law, was permitted to exist apart from municipal jurisdiction, although it is a part of London, not far from the Inns of Court. It is a city within a city, a nation within a nation, a foreign country inhabited by London's outlaws. It has its criminal morality, its own laws and language, the cant of thieves which critics have found so amusing. When Tim escapes from his imprisonment in the country while his father is abroad on business, he comes directly to Alsatia, a rebel to William's tyrannic paternal government. The opening scene shows him perfectly duped by the fleecers who indoctrinate him into his new free life of wine and women. He finds delight in their crass jargon which he calls witty. He considers them his dear friends because they freely bestow upon him fine clothes and slovenly women. Of course, their plan is to make him pay fully for these pleasures. He enjoys a respite from his father's tyranny, but the comedy of his freedom rests on our awareness that he will soon be as much at the mercy of his new guides as he was at the mercy of Sir William, and that he will be less free than he ever was if they succeed in ruining him.

The Alsatian gang, an index to villainy in Shadwellian comedy, embodies varieties of criminal "humors." Cheatly, the gang's mastermind, is a loquacious instructor in crime, dissembling friendship and protecting himself when opposed by releasing a smoke screen of legalistic double-talk. Below him are Shamwell and Hackum, who share Cheatly's cowardice, but whose tactics differ from his. Shamwell, Tim's cousin, lured the clod into the Alsatian web. Once rich, Shamwell was fleeced in London, and he wants to recoup his losses by fleecing his kin. Such an unnatural attitude toward kin, Shadwell explored most deeply in *The Miser;* but in *The Squire* he draws startling parallels between Cousin Shamwell's use of Tim as prey and Father William's use of Tim as filial slave. William's cruelty is like Shamwell's, but their motives and methods differ. Captain Hackum belongs to Shadwell's gallery of rowdies and braggart warriors, types which he developed fully in his penultimate comedy, *The Scowrers.* After deserting the army, unpatriotic Hackwell "retreated into *White-fryers*" and earned a living cheating fools who wandered into it, with the aid of his wife who supplies fuel for fools, cherry brandy and prostitutes, Betty and Margaret.

When Ned extricates Tim from the Alsatian trap at the end of the play, and after the criminals are arrested, the usually calm Sir Edward vigorously denounces the city within the city. He underscores Alsatia's emblematic significance as a place of rebellion and so implies that Ned's destruction of some of its citizens is a real service to England: "Was ever such impudence suffered in Government? *Ireland*'s Conquer'd: *Wales* Subdu'd: *Scotland* United: But there are some few spots of Ground in *London,* just in the face of the Government, unconquer'd yet, that hold in Rebellion still. Methinks 'tis strange, that places so near the Kings Palace should be no part of his Dominions. . . ." Ned's victory is a public one, expressing social and political ideals of order and justice which Shadwell associated with the Glorious Revolution. It is also great proof of the value of a liberal education which can teach the extent of personal freedom and the limitations of revolt and crime.

Alsatians can dupe only those so blinded by dullness that they cannot penetrate the false masks of friendship. Alsatians thrive upon illusions of promises of joy and freedom for men who have never been free. But Alsatia is not the only place in London harboring criminals. There are other villains who exploit unwary victims by assuming socially acceptable guises. Such a villain is Scrapeall, the Puritanical usurer who sponsors the fleecing of Tim, who moves freely between London and the Alsatian world. He hides his criminality in his special language, religious cant; and he shows what Shadwell's hypocritical Puritans always show: a penchant for dovetailing religious zeal and money-making under the guise of a Protestant ethic of wealth. Like the Alsatians, he is ironically a source of Ned's triumph. Ned and his friend Truman fall in love with Scrapeall's niece Isabella and his daughter Teresia, and Scrapeall is a blocking character whom the youths must outwit. Scrapeall's restrictions describe another of the educational modes presented in the play. His approach is like Sir William's, but it is marked by irredeemable malice. William wants Tim to be a good son, the comfort of his age, but Scrapeall is concerned only with keeping the girls chaste so that they can be more lucratively sold as brides. Lacking any moral sense, he shares with Shamwell a consciously unnatural attitude toward kin, although he is not pressed into crime by poverty.

Mrs. Termagant, Ned's cast-off mistress, also links Alsatia and London. She moves between them, trying to transplant White-friar villainy to a London which is essentially non-criminal—or, at least, which has laws that safeguard virtuous people. Over-bearingly emotional, melodramatic, and aggressive, she resembles the amazonian villainesses of heroic plays, and her morbid hysteria modifies the comic tone of the play in scenes where she is a key figure. Her sole end is to win back Ned who, she claims, has fathered her baby girl. In Act III, she inaugurates a series of plots which show her inexhaustible potential for re-venge. First, she disguises herself as Ned's abandoned wife, hop-ing thus to turn Isabella against him; later she dresses as a male and claims to be Isabella's husband, hoping to turn Ned against Isabella. When these plots fail, she resorts to violence, first by attempting to stab Ned and then (nearly creating a tragedy out of a comedy) by firing a pistol point-blank at him. Like her plots, the pistol flashes in the pan. Indeed, all the anxiety she creates in Ned's life convinces him that marriage and a settled life will bring him peace of mind. In Act V, she surrenders her baby to Sir Edward who promises to "breed her up and provide for her like a Gentlewoman." The successful educator will be-gin again to pass on his influence to a new generation.

Ned Belfond makes his first appearance at the beginning of Act II, immediately after he has deflowered Lucia, the well-bred daughter of his father's attorney. Shadwell presents Lucia in a sympathetic way, hardly typical of the approach to the seduced girl in Restoration drama. He does not direct comic criticism at her as he does toward Termagant, nor does he ask us to damn her for her morally unforgivable and socially unwise sin of losing her maidenhead before winning her husband. Lucia regrets her sin, but she is a girl in love; Ned's "Flattering Tongue" and "Bewitching Eyes" were as irresistible as the Devil's when he seduced Eve—or so the imagery of their dialogue indicates. As part of Termagant's revenge, she informs Lucia's father of the affair. When he confronts his daughter and, shocked and miser-able, reminds her of her indulgent and careful education, it is clear that this father-child relationship is intended as yet another variation on the main theme of education in *The Squire*. In this instance perhaps liberalism failed. At any rate, Lucia is not socially punished for her sin. In the final scenes, Shadwell recognizes the claims of the female in a man's world where, for men, pre-marital promiscuity is not a crime.

When in Act IV, Williams learns of Ned's dastardly seduction of "sweet" Lucia, he loses all respect for him. To Edward's promise that reparation will be provided for the ruined girl, William wisely and comically asks, "Reparation, for making his Daughter a Whore! What, a Pox, can he give her her Maiden-head again?" In *The Squire,* this rhetorical question has a positive answer, and the answer is directly related to Ned's growing awareness of the damage he has done to Lucia. He lies about the affair, swearing publicly that he has *not* seduced her and so restores, if not her virtue, at least her reputation. This lie is the price he must pay to give her back "her Maiden-head"— actually the greatest price he can pay; for he is proud, above all, of his truthfulness to Edward. The lie constitutes a surrender of his integrity, as from another point of view, it deflates his pride and helps to make him a complete gentleman: a man willing to tarnish his character in order to save the pathetic girl. In the comic world of perplexing entanglements, Ned's heroic triumph is qualified by the lie.

Ned's libertinism, expressed in a conversation with Truman, makes clear the philosophical basis of his actions. He never wholly abandons his philosophy, even in Act V, yet his misadventures convince him to modify it. He and Truman find society absurd: all the joys "we can invent, are little enough to make the Farce of Life go down"; most men keep busy, are "grave and wise, about this Life, as if there were something in it," while "Wise men know there's nothing to be done here but to make the best of a bad Market." Ned's education appears to have made him a nihilist, contemptuous of society, who wiles away his hours enjoying the pleasures of food, wine, music, and literature, particularly of his favorite authors, Horace and Shakespeare. For a rake, his love life is complete: he has enjoyed the extremes of womankind, a tempestuous mistress and a tender virgin. He does not forsee in this early act that forces are emerging in his life which will alter, if not his philosophy, at least his aimlessness. Various persons will impinge upon his career— his brother, his father, his uncle, his ex-mistress, his virgin, his true love Isabella. Together they will shatter his easy existence, lift him out of his complacency, and bind him firmly to society. Ned does not find life more meaningful at the end, but life compels him to act as if it were.

Sir Edward grows disturbed over Ned's failure to begin living up to the great ideals of a liberal education. Rakehellism was to have been but a stage in the process of growth, but Edward fears that Ned's insatiable passion and insouciance have become an end. He sternly warns his nephew that "there's nothing but Anxiety in Vice," that he "ne'r knew any thing gotten by Wenching, but Duels, Claps, and Bastards: And every drunken fit is a short madness, that cuts off a good part of Life." Ned admires Sir Edward, and he comprehends the educational ideal, but the advice is not enough to convert him.

Advice is a guide; other factors have greater power to influence his conversion. Termagant's harassment convinces him that a rake's life is a "foolish, restless, anxious life; and there's an end on't." But running from her histrionics, he plunges into new adventures which create different kinds of anxiety. Lucia merely flatters his masculine ego; she cannot redirect him toward worthy action. This is Isabella's role. She represents a harmonious vision to which he can aspire only if he channels his vast energies for constructive purposes. He and Truman become knights-errant determined to rescue Isabella and her cousin, damsels in distress, from Scrapeall's despotism. Ned removes Isabella from Scrapeall's domain and carries her to the sanctuary of Sir Edward's house where, unlike the sanctuary of Alsatia, she will receive fair treatment and be free. Her salvation is also his. Although he loses his bachelor-freedom in freeing her, he also loses his anxiety. Marriage becomes an event which, he prophesies, will make his journey through life less confusing, more meaningful.

Tim Belfond also supplies Ned with a specific reason for positive action. In their first encounter in Alsatia, Ned sees Tim "Transmography'd" from a country fool to a city dupe. Kinship inspires him to join Sir William in a righteous war against Alsatia, and the aim is to redeem Tim. The various defeats of Termagant, Cheatly, Shamwell, Hackum, and Scrapeall are essential to the achievement of the various victories of Lucia, Isabella, Teresia, William, Edward, Truman, Tim, and, of course, Ned. The victors join together in the concluding joyous dance, and not unlike the hero of the sentimental plays of the eighteenth century, Ned bids a somber "long farewell to all the Vanity and Lewdness of Youth," offering himself as a "Sacrifice without a blemish now" to Isabella.

This view of himself is ironic and his expectations of an anxiety-free life in marriage are also ironic. Will it be easy for Ned to become his wife's submissive slave? Despite his several redemptive acts, he is not a "Sacrifice without a Blemish." And there is enough to suggest that marriage may be a temporary retreat from life's confusions, and that, when he discovers his new responsibilities, his new-found joy will be short-lived. Sir Edward wisely avoided matrimonial entanglements. Sir William admits that he hated his wife. In such ways the sentimental mood of Ned's surrender to Hymen is qualified. In the last two comedies, *The Scowrers* and *The Volunteers*, Shadwell returned to the sentimental reformation of the rake, but he offered few doubts as to the dangers of wedlock and its restrictions on the individual hero.[4]

II *The Fair at Bury*

Bury-Fair surveys again the world as a market place where a hero must learn to purchase the best that is available to him. It studies the extent to which a wit can control his "humor" and his environment, and it bases its action implicitly on modes of education and ways of approaching society. In many ways, it reminds us of Shadwell's earliest comedies, *The Sullen Lovers* and *The Humorists,* with their rhapsodical fools pitting their "humors" against the witty characters. According to the London wit Wildish, Bury "is really a sweet Town"; but its sweetness is alloyed by flocks of fashionable and unfashionable people who remind him of London's dullards—the effeminate Trim, who denies man's bestial nature in his showers of nauseous politesse; the Fantasts, mother and daughter, whose preciosity and pedantry corrupt Bury's simple atmosphere; the crude practical joker Sir Humphrey Noddy and the blustering Oldwit who have no sense of refinement. This "numerous, Impudent, and Noisy Party" are attracted to the annual Fair to which come also the happy few, "Modest and Reserv'd. . . . Men of Wit, Honour, and Breeding; and Women of great Wit, Beauty, and Ingenuity, and Well-bred too." Among such women are Oldwit's two daughters, sentimental Philadelphia and sharp-tongued Gertrude (Gatty). Among the men are Wildish, the city rake, and his friend Lord Bellamy, the reformed rake who has retired to the country.

At first, Shadwell makes it difficult for us to decide which of the two men he considers the hero. Both are libertines; both claim to have solved the problem of coping with impertinence and of living the good life; yet their solutions are entirely different. More strikingly than any of Shadwell's heroes, Wildish embodies characteristics which contemporary playgoers admired in their comic heroes. He is a satirist by profession, sardonic, witty, and wise. He has come to Bury to pursue Gatty, but he loathes Bury society which he conveniently divides into two classes of dullness: foppery and crudeness. The first type is marked by facile pastoralism, false heroic ideals, and Frenchified manners and snobbery. The second is merely vulgar—even despite crude Oldwit's claim that he learned his wit from his old drinking companions, Jonson, Fletcher, and Cleveland.

Through Wildish's brittle wit, we observe the fools of *Bury-Fair,* and we join him in his satiric plot (his "Admirable Farce") by means of which he plans to expose the more abhorrent witlessness, the effete pretensions of the Fantasts to fashion and learning. He fabricates an intrigue by hiring the French periwig maker, La Roch, to impersonate a count. Like Congreve's Mirabel or Shaw's Professor Higgins, Wildish intends passing off a false aristocrat in a society which cannot distinguish between a man and his appearance. The plot titillates his satiric sense, but his primary aim is to bring Gatty back to London as his wife.

He rebukes Bellamy for leaving London. It has its clowns, but it has also its worthy men with whom a true wit can fashion a reasonably satisfactory life in a highly unsatisfactory universe. Wildish's commentary resolves in part the ambiguous Augustan attitude toward the city and civilization. London is corrupt, offering the *worst* that civilization has to offer. But it is also the dynamic center of artistic, scientific, and political action; and, as such, it contains and perpetuates the great urban tradition. London's variety permits a wise man to arrange "artistically" his life by enjoying and preserving what he considers meaningful. Bury offers little in the way of variety, and truly wise men cannot enjoy intelligent life in such a limited environment.

Bellamy insists, however, that he has enjoyed such a life. Before the play opened, he quit London and, with stoic resignation, carried with him, as part of his cultural baggage, the *best* of the great urban tradition—fine music, books, ideas. He kept his privacy, made a few close friends, and avoided the many rural "Birds and Cattel." Not far from Bury he created an "illusion" of ideal country living. But Bellamy does not deny the basic ugliness of humanity as do Trim and the Fantasts, the other creators of illusion in the play who pretend that man is a pastoral shepherd or a superhuman tragic hero. Yet Bellamy feels that London makes the ugliness seem harsher. London is a crammed jungle, with "So many Pens of Wild Beasts upon two Legs, undermining, lying in wait, preying upon, informing against, and hanging one another," all "Noise and Nonsense."

Against this familiar satiric view of London, Wildish shows the real differences between Bellamy and himself. He believes that man "was made a Sociable Animal"; not being "self-sufficient," man expresses himself more fully through such social pleasures as friendship, love, and even satire. To Wildish, Bellamy's isolationism is a denial of human nature—an accusation which Bellamy resents. Bellamy calls his friend a "Slave" to the tyranny of nature and society because he lets his life be determined by natural-social passions. The Fair and its human comedy are a perfect setting in which the friends test the validity of their self-satisfied ideas. And, although they never deny these ideas, somber, somewhat pretentious Bellamy and satiric, frivolous Wildish are taken down a peg by the girls marvellously matched to them—serious Philadelphia Oldwit and candid, honest Gatty Oldwit.

Bellamy, coming to Bury to "raffle his heart" to Gatty, is accompanied by his new servant Charles, who is really Philadelphia in disguise (a situation reminiscent of *Twelfth Night* or *The Plain Dealer*). Philadelphia fled from her father's house because he planned marrying her to a fop. Like Gatty, she has a spunky love of liberty, but there is far more sweetness than light, more pathos in her personality than in Gatty's. For all his assertions of perceptiveness, Bellamy is totally fooled by her disguise, a fact which (according to Gatty) is serious enough to disqualify him as her suitor. Gatty's heart has been secretly palpitating for Wildish long before, but he presents problems to her. She cherishes candidness, but to win him she must learn to dissemble. She makes him go the way of all reformable rakes, however, by bluntly feigning abhorrence to marriage. Her rural seriousness, her hatred of frivolity for its own sake, and her high sense of independence demand that he adopt a sobriety hitherto unknown to him. He must modify his view of life as a satiric joke; but she laughs with him at the fools and plays observer as well as actor in the social comedy, much like Lovel and Carolina in *The Sullen Lovers.* Because the heroine chooses Wildish, he emerges as the hero. Bellamy, in contrast, seems "unstable," particularly when, after discovering Philadelphia's identity, he switches his affection from Gatty to this melting girl who mirrors perfectly his own sentimental sobriety.

In this play, more subtly than in *Epsom* and the *Witches,* Shadwell relates symbolically the setting of the Fair to the meaning of the central action. The Fair is the *raison d'être* for drawing together the characters. Two scenes (II, ii and IV, ii) are devoted to it. The first points up parallels between the vendors who cry their wares and the characters who come to buy and sell their personalities and emotions—in short, themselves—in the market place of love and marriage. Gatty draws attention to the Fair's significance: "'Tis pleasant to observe the mixture of People here" and she means not only the barking vendors and unidentified *"People walking up and down,"* but also the major characters of the play. When her half-sister Mrs. Fantast scorns the *"Canaille"* of the Fair, Gatty swiftly retorts with her tolerant views of humanity. She praises the "common People" of Bury who, without the arts and affectations of civilization, stay close to Nature. Civilization, not Nature, creates *canaille,* fools. Her view restates Shadwell's theory of "humors" characters: "humors" are like Mrs. Fantast who has assiduously metamorphosed herself into a caricature. "Humors" come to the Fair to expose their "artfully" created folly. But they fool only themselves and other fools.

The Fair is actually a center for civilized fools. Its merchants do not sell the vital necessities but the luxuries of life—massy plate, *"Portugal* sweets to burn in your Chamber," "very rich *Indian* stuffs," "Fine mellow Pears," and "very good Gingerbread." The perfumer's cries are emblematic of the Fair and they point ambiguously to its larger meaning: "What d'ye lack? What d'ye buy?"—What emotional or social joys are you seeking? This larger meaning is also suggested when Sir Humphrey (Trim's rival for Mrs. Fantast's hand) offers her a gift:

> *Sir Humphrey.* Madam, let me present you with your first Fairing, a Heart.
> *Gertrude.* Of Ginger-bread.
> *Sir Humphrey.* Ay faith, pretty Lady.
> *Gertrude.* Is it a true Image of your own? Did you sit for it?
> *Sir Humphrey.* Ha, ha, ha; a very good Jest! Udsbud, there's a pair of Gloves of the same mettle, to stop your pretty Mouth. And, Mr. *Trim,* here is a Wise Cap [of gingerbread], befitting your Gravity, and the Solidity of your Parts, for you.

Gatty wants a real, profoundly affectionate heart. When Bellamy gallantly proposes a raffle of hearts, she abstains. Love should not be a capricious gamble, a Fair game. When she wins Wildish, who excited her heart at the Fair, she exchanges with him a precious possession, her hand (her freedom) for his heart (his freedom and feelings).

The dissembling of Gatty and Philadelphia to win their loves is sharply contrasted to the other kind of dissembling which informs Bury's social life and which is the major theme of the La Roch-Fantast affair. This affair brings together the two kinds of deception in the play, the conscious and the unconscious (in which deceivers fool only themselves). Wildish shrewdly chooses La Roch to play the role of Monsieur le Count de Cheveux, for this Frenchman thrives upon deception as a manufacturer of wigs, symbols of disguise. Transforming him into a nobleman is an easy task. Bury's ladies lionize him. Mrs. Fantast falls instantly under his spell—even though her mother boasts that she educated her to draw sharp lines between the beau monde and *canaille.* In the witty conversation in Act II between La Roch and the Fantasts, distinctions between appearance and reality are proliferated into a series of comic gag lines. Old Lady Fantast, whose face her husband Oldwit calls a wall which she fills with cosmetics "as House-painters do the Cracks in Wainscot, with Putty," is flattered inordinately when La Roch feigns surprise that she is the mother and not the sister of Mrs. Fantast: "Begar, Madam, den you be de pretty Modere, she de pretty Daughtere, in de whole Varle. Oh mine Art, mine Art! . . . I broughtè de Arte out of *France,* and I ave lost it in dis plas: is gone, Madam; an Morbleau, you see now de French Count vidout a Heart."

In his lines, La Roch persistently reveals his duplicity. He is a man without a "heart"—or a man whose heart is not real, only a fabrication created by "art," by lies. He often lets slip his mask, for he cannot totally hide his professional passions. He praises Mrs. Fantast's hair, "dose tresses [which] Conquer de Lovere," the kind of hair which Cupid makes his net of "to catchè de Art." If he had her hair, he "wou'd makè two tree Peruke of dat." Oldwit reminds him that he is not a barber, yet such gross negligence of his aristocrat manner creates no suspicion in the women who want to believe that a French count admires them.

Like the characters in *The Humorists,* the Fantasts rush headlong toward their social deaths. Mrs. Fantast agrees to wed the false count, but when La Roch decides to go through with the marriage, Wildish swiftly exposes him and, consequently, the Fantasts. The Fantasts become the laughing stock of Bury society, the scapegoats of country pretensions. Their friends, the ladies of Bury, insist that they were not deceived by La Roch. But the incident will not change them; country pretensions will continue to thrive.

As in *The Humorists* and *Epsom-Wells,* the engagements of the four lovers are celebrated as a contrapuntal action to Oldwit's "great Deliverance"—the dissolution of his marriage to the incorrigible Lady Fantast. He does not understand the sentimentalism of Bellamy and Philadelphia or the sharp wit of Wildish and Gatty, but he senses the excellence of their characters. The sincerity of the first pair and the sardonic impulses of the second seem to approximate more closely his old Jonsonian attitudes toward plain-dealing satire than all of his wife's preciousness. Oldwit insists that they "Revel for a Month at least" and that their revelry be a public affair, an appropriate climax to the Fair: "Let all this Night be spent in Mirth, and Wine,/Let's lose no part of it in beastly Sleep."

III *A Note on Shadwell's Language*

In *The Squire* and *Bury-Fair,* Shadwell repeatedly calls our attention to language, to its varieties, to its way of concealing or revealing character, to its nature as a communicating instrument which can inform the perceptive listener of certain truths and certain lies—truths and lies which the imperceptive listener cannot discern. More than in his other comedies, peculiarities of speech and style are closely related to character development.

Something of the significance of language in these plays has been described above—in Ned Belfond's great lie concerning Lucia's innocence and in La Roch's speeches which deceive only the foolish ladies of Bury. In each case, language is a kind of smoke screen that fools some people. It is closely related, however, to the major themes of the play—to Ned's heroic sacrifice and to the explosion of Bury's pretensions.

Perhaps Shadwell's wittiest treatment of language occurs in the Fantasts' dialogues which are reminiscent of Sir Formal Trifle's florid oratory in *The Virtuoso.* But the satire on ornate style in *Bury* has a special impact because it is directed at the kind of women whom Shadwell rarely depicts: those who cannot control the world they live in, who do not triumph. Trapped by their intellectualism, their pedantic learning, they are sharply contrasted to the unintellectual, but wisely intuitive Gatty. They impress their naïve maid Luce, but Gatty detests their circumlocutory Latinate style artificially sprinkled with French *mots.* In Act II we find the three together for the first time:

Mrs. Fantast.   Sweet Madam *Gatty,* I have some Minutes impatiently expected your arrival, that I might do my self the great Honour to kiss your Hands, and enjoy the favour of your Company into the Fair; which I see, out of my Window, begins to fill apace.

Gertrude.   I got ready as soon as e're I cou'd, and am now come to wait on you.

Lady Fantast.   Oh, fye, [step] Daughter! will you never attain, by mine, and my dear Daughters Examples, to a more Polite way of Expression, and a Nicer form of Breeding? Fye, fye, . . . You shou'd have said; I assure you, Madam, the honour is all on my side, and I cannot be ambitious of a greater, than the enjoyment of the sweet Society of so excellent a Person. This is Breeding.

This is, also, for Gatty, lying. She dislikes the Fantasts as much as they dislike her. Their smoke screen of flowery compliment perverts communication and makes painfully verbose the simplest expression. According to Jean Gagen, the Fantasts are examples of what she calls the "learned lady"—not featherbrained women, but serious pretenders to knowledge who have an ample intellectual background.[5] Yet, without formal learning, Gatty displays a deeper knowledge of life, as for example, in her remarks on language: "Conversation," she insists, "ought to be free, easie, and natural." Nationalistically, she defends her native tongue: true English women, wives and mothers, do not need Latin or French to maintain successfully their households. Her dicta and maxims outline an admirable ideal of clear style and thinking which, in turn, reflects the wisdom of the speaker who does not need ornaments to conceal realities.

Like the Fantasts, Trim hides his dullness behind the images and style of a moribund pastoralism. He is Eugenius exchanging poems with his literary Dorinda, Mrs. Fantast. By trying thus to lose his identity, he denies its worth. Pastoral language is intended to make him more attractive than he actually is; instead, it proves how unattractive he really is, and it demonstrates his failure to adjust to the truths of his vacuous personality.

The examples of the Fantasts and Trim should not suggest, however, that the masks which language can provide are to be eschewed in Shadwell's comic world. Even Gatty must learn to conceal her feelings for Wildish so that she can win him. To state these feelings frankly would be to become an immodest female. She would lose her "mystery" for Wildish. Philadelphia also speaks a disguising language as a male page to hide her sex, her courage, love, and fidelity from Bellamy. Beneath the superficial linguistic embellishments of the pretentious people, we are hard put to find real worth; beneath the dissembling wit and style of the worthier characters, we recognize something finer, something which cannot, ultimately, be expressed in a simple way.

This double nature of language as an instrument that reveals or that hides truths rests at the very core of the meaning of *The Squire*. The Alsatians have their foreign comic language. A newcomer, who hopes to live in this underworld of double-dealers, must learn an entirely different way of expressing himself. The crucial scenes, when the dupers instruct Tim Belfond in Alsatian cant, show us the difference between plain English (direct, often witty, always clear and meaningful) and the smoke screen of jargon reflecting the tireless concerns of rogues and derelicts. Money is their most important word, and they have numerous synonyms for it: *cole, ready, rhino, darby.* A rich man is *rhino-cerical.* A second concern, lust, gives many names to prostitutes and mistresses—*blowings, naturals, convenients, tackles, buttocks, pure,* and *purest pure.* Tim thinks these are all "the prettiest witty words," and by Act III he has mastered the essentials and become "A thorough-pac'd *White-Friers* man." But Alsatian is a simple language, actually a degenerate offshoot of plain speech, and not far from this cant are the dull sounds of animals. The master criminal Cheatly teaches Tim to avoid conversation alto-gether by pulling his hat down and by answering bothersome questions with a vapid "Bow wow."

Cheatly is an expert when it comes to perverting the com-municating instrument. To survive as a criminal he knows that he must mask constantly his criminal intentions. Besides cant and the sounds of animals, he resorts to "bantering"—circumlocutions and padding to bury truth. He banters Lolpoop, the clod who in-sists that Tim quit Alsatia, so: "Your Master being in this matter, to deport his Count'nance somewhat obliquely, to some prin-ciples, which others but out of a Mature Gravity may have weigh'd, and think too heavy to be undertaken! what does it avail you if you shall precipitate or plunge yourself into affairs, as unsuitable to your Physnomy as they are to your Com-plexion [?]" Shadwell also satirizes legal jargon through Cheatly who sprinkles liberally *Scire facias, Nisi Prius, Non est inventus* and similar terms into his uncommunicative communications. The criminal is well acquainted with the legal double-talk and knows how to use it to create confusions among the uninitiated.

Lolpoop, an easy victim of Alsatian smoke screens, has yet his own language, the limited North Country dialect so distinct in its clumsiness from the straightforward English of a Sir Edward or a Ned Belfond. Scrapeall's Puritanical cant is another kind of language in *The Squire*, a "*Canaantish* Dialect" which conceals his very unchristian spirit. Ned and Truman, disguised as Puritans in their secret rendezvous with Isabella and Teresia, come, as Ned says, mimicking Scrapeall, "to confer with thee, in

a matter which concerneth us both"; this style is sustained even
as he tries seducing Isabella, for "Something within me whis-
pereth, that we were made as helps for one another." But
Isabella, like Gatty, hates hypocritical circumlocution. "Come,"
she demands, "leave off your *Canaantish* Dialect, and talk like
Inhabiters of this World," "talk like Gentlemen."

Isabella is naïve, however. She does not know that gentleman's
talk is not necessarily the equivalent of plain style, that it is
really an instrument for complex thought, more so than any of
the other styles of *The Squire*. It can, as she hopes, state ideas
straightforwardly. It can express philosophy. It can play brightly
with the oxymoronic paradoxes of libertinism where debauchery
is "honest." It can lie if necessary to save a reputation. It can
express plain truth in a polished way. It can ask for a hand in
marriage. It can redeem the past by promising a brighter future.
In short, it can be the finest linguistic instrument for the man
who can control it wisely. Ned, who respects the power of the
instrument, controls it. Characters like Sir William and Mrs.
Termagant let their emotions run away with them; they are
controlled by language. Sometimes, even gentleman's talk is not
perfect; it may create *malentendues*. When Sir William mistakes
reports of Tim's misadventures for Ned's misadventures, language
is a primary source of confusion. It can be an instrument—an
inadequate one—for Mrs. Termagant's endless lies, spoken in
plain English, which show how easily plain English can express
deceit. Only Sir Edward in *The Squire* does not use language to
deceive, hide, or to gain selfish ends. He speaks the language of
an honest man, sincere without frenzy, wise without pride,
absolved even from the sin of lying which qualifies the hero's
triumph.

CHAPTER 8

Last Plays

THE educational theme, so pertinent in *The Squire* and *Bury-Fair,* concerned Shadwell deeply in his late years. In the Dedication of *The Amorous Bigotte,* he insisted that "the most important business of this world, the Education of Youth" (because it brings no worthy "Rewards and Dignities" to the ablest persons) is "put upon such mean, weak, or corrupt persons, that it is the greatest task of a mans life to break loose from his Education, and shake off the prejudices he contracted by it; which none but a great *Genius* ever does." Typically, Shadwell adapted these and other serious reflections on education to the comic mode where he could satirically qualify them, whether he was thinking of the result of so doubtful a *genius* as cloddish Tim Belfond or the wiser revolts of the two Spanish maidens, Elvira and Rosania in *The Amorous Bigotte.* In this farcical treatment of the educational theme, Shadwell makes it clear that genius means common sense, a strong will, and an undying desire to be free. For young girls, it includes the impulse to marry the man of one's choice.

There are many such young geniuses in Shadwell's plays, but wise mentors are few. Sir Edward in *The Squire* is exceptional, and it is part of Ned's education to recognize this fact fully. In the Dedication, Shadwell singled out two characteristics necessary in a youth who wishes to revolt successfully, "strength of Understanding, and industrious Enquiry." Nature gave these characteristics to youths to prevent them from obeying the fallacious dicta of bad guides—a Lady Busy, a Cheatly or Shamwell, a Lady Fantast. But there were also those not so graced by nature who "tho of the highest rank, swallow every thing unchew'd, and take every thing unexamin'd from their first Dry-Nurses in Petticoats to their last in Square-Caps; Women begin with them, and young Priests end with 'em. . . ."

These two great centers of false education, the maternal and the ecclesiastical, are the special satiric targets in *The Amorous Bigotte,* its subtitle—*with the Second Part of Tegue O Divelly*—reminding us that the comedy is a sequel to *The Lancashire Witches.*[1] Belliza, the lady of the title, is a widow who is torn between the desires of this world and the heavenly promises of the other. Her inability to decide which world she really wants makes her an unstable guide for her sensible daughter Elvira and for her virtuous but not very intelligent niece Rosania. They declare against Belliza and strive successfully to win their heroes and to enjoy the pleasures of *this* world.

Other incompetent educators inhabit Shadwell's Madrid, where the action occurs. Don Bernardo, the blustering army officer and father of the chivalric Luscindo, falls madly in love first with Belliza, then with Elvira, and finally again with Belliza, after his son wins Elvira. Bernardo is headstrong, unstable, crude. Luscindo can learn from him only what a wise man should *not* be. Gremia is another poor guide. As head of a bawdy house, she constantly protests that she has taught her girls not only the lucrative art of love but, being a strict observer of Catholic ritual, the proper adoration of the Church. She supports the devil in business, but under no conditions can she be tempted to eat meat on a fish day. And the last figure in this group of educators is Father Tegue, whose lust and hypocrisy are as intense as they were when we first met him in *The Lancashire Witches.*

There is very little subtlety in this satire on Catholicism and on lust in the older characters. Their actions and personalities are blatantly farcical. And it would not take much of a genius to recognize their equivocal approaches to life. Tegue's attempts to rape Rosania teach her instantaneously that he is no moral guide. When Bernardo asks Belliza to marry him and when she gives up her firm religious vow never to remarry, Elvira gives her up as a steady guide. What kind of truth can Belliza offer when, at the least provocation, she alters her entire approach to living? And what counter-education is available to a girl like Elvira in a world cluttered with unstable hypocrites and sensualists? She reads Cervantes' *Nouvellas Ejemplas* and spends hours gazing into her pocket mirror—two great sins, according to her bigoted mother. She learns the value of dropping her handkerchief as a lure for Luscindo. She independently plans a rendezvous with him. She has, in short, no direct answer to bigotry and restrictions. She can only follow her normal feminine impulses and trust in her personal sense of virtue. Gazing at herself in the mirror, entranced by her own beauty, wanting to use physical attractions to trap Luscindo who can liberate her from Belliza, she teaches herself, comically and romantically, to "know herself," to accept the reality of her desires. She educates herself simply by realizing that she wants to be free.

In the sweltering Spanish atmosphere with its "mad" confusions and farcical intrigues, many *malentendues*, cross-purposes, misplaced letters, misleading rendezvous, lies and counter-lies, everything happens at so frantic a pace that it becomes a triumph simply to survive the confusion and to emerge sane and married by the end of the play. The educational lesson of *The Amorous Bigotte*, then, is that youth is self-reliant, innately and wonderfully prone to finding its heart's desire. In a world without educators and *raisonneurs*, in a place like Catholic Spain, youthful naïveté, with perhaps a touch of dissembling, is the best guide, the best key to survival.

The setting of the last two plays is London and although, as my brief treatment of them will show, they incorporate many of the characters, situations, and themes which Shadwell employed from his earliest plays, each has that rare figure in Shadwell's comic universe—an elderly man who is wise and who directly influences the young people: Mr. Rant in *The Scowrers* and Major General Blunt in *The Volunteers, or The Stock-Jobbers*. Both men are country persons who bring with them to London, a foolish city, the sane wisdom of the retired life. They are, in different ways, sententious moralists, but not maudlin sentimentalists. Blunt explicitly decries sentimentality, but, like Rant, he demands candor and earthy honesty. Both are highly emotional when it comes to praising the good life which they embody.

I *The Enemy at Home*

Remembering Shadwell's belief that worthy youths will revolt against bad educators and that most educators are bad, it is clear that he freighted the conflicts of *The Scowrers* with ironies. The youth in this play is Sir William Rant, a notorious critic of society who is in violent and ironic revolt against a father and an education which were *not* bad. This "genius" is the head of a fraternity of scowrers which, according to W. H. Irving, "may conceivably have been at first a voluntary organization to help the watch preserve order. . . . At any rate, they soon degenerated into clubs of drunken rake-hells amusing themselves at the expense of harmless people."[2] Among the scowrers, William has found a second father, Old Tope, a good-natured man-about-town of the "last age" who initiates William and his friend Wildfire into the mysteries of London debauchery. Tope pretends to be as young as his pupils, the man who can never become serious about life, law, and order.

William is idealized by three minor scowrers—Whackum and two Alsatian bullies Bluster and Dingboy—who lack the finesse of the gentlemanly scowrers. All of them, however, are destructive—they break windows, create nightly rumpuses, beat citizens and constables, do anything which *overtly* states their loathing of conventional life. But there are obvious differences between William and his crude imitators. His revolt is based on libertine principles. The others, mere rowdies, base their action on no philosophic ideas.

The comedy traces the steps by which the hero represses his lust for disorder and not only accepts but admires the gentler, selfless wisdom of Mr. Rant. In the opening scene, Sir William, attired in a morning gown, groggily tries to remember what happened during another of his nightly drinking bouts, "the latter part" being "all Darkness." The reference to darkness is the first of many suggestions that he is a demoniac power, a Prince of Darkness who holds morning court in his apartment and pontificates on libertinism. Friends, creditors, and courtesans (Mavis and Haughty) flock to see him. His servant Ralph describes disapprovingly his flaw with disarming simplicity: he is a "hot Head." But Sir William believes that his evening was "very handsomely spent" as a law-enforcing gadfly impressing dullards with the realities of human animalism and destructiveness. He is Shadwell's angriest young man, neither a dupe like Sir Humphrey Scattergood nor a villain like Don John, although he resembles both.

Among this devil's visitors is Sir Humphrey Maggot, a country relative who is visiting London with a lubricious wife and his daughters by a former marriage, Eugenia and Clara. Sir Humphrey delivers a letter from Mr. Rant, but William impiously tears it up. He wanted money, but received instead "a parcel of wise Council that is not worth a Farthing." Rant blasts his son for his vicious prodigality and is especially disturbed over the news that William has impregnated the Parson's daughter—one of several girls who have been tempted by this devil and fallen in the headlong sweep of his satanic progress.

Yet, as is usual in the Shadwell hero, there is enough to indicate that William can enact a moral hero's part. Compared to Sir Humphrey Maggot, he is at least shrewd enough to know that most people are fools or criminals. The seduction of the Parson's daughter is typical of his manner of "scowrering" society, for *she* should have been, by her father's example, immune to his demonism. Sir Humphrey (a character modeled perhaps after Jonson's Sir Politick Would-be in *Volpone*) is so concerned with foreign events that he fails to consider serious domestic problems such as the fact that his wife is trying to cuckold him. He fares no better as an educator than he does as a husband. As young Whackum's mentor, he thinks that Whackum is studying hard in the Inns of Court when, indeed, this bully's only studies are to be as great a scowrer as William.

The hero and his best friend Wildfire fall in love with Eugenia and Clara Maggot, but they are overwhelmed to find themselves confronted not with some melting Parson's daughter nor with a submissive courtesan, but with two Shadwellian females who are also in the process of revolting by defying their stepmother who is herself defying the law (of marriage) in her pursuit of Wildfire. Wildfire, who ultimately tricks Lady Maggot, forces her by blackmail to let him and William marry the girls. Eugenia and Clara scorn their bad educator. In Act II, they defy their humorous guard Priscilla by running off to Hyde Park in search of city sparks who can liberate them from Lady Maggot's bondage. In the Park, a patch of country in the heart of the city,[3] they declare their naturalistic rights of independence as "true English Women, Co-heirs of two thousand pounds a year," and they resolve to "assert our Liberty and Property" by throwing off the "Yoke of Arbitrary power, under which we have so long groan'd." Theirs is a Glorious Revolution in the London of William and Mary which they call a "Paradice of the world," the

locale of their rebirth and salvation after a dreary country existence, a "most blessed Town" with "heavenly walks." But in this
Paradise they meet the devil William and his friend.

Clara, the more rational of the pair, is quick, however, to
sense a touch of self-destruction in her sister's lust for liberty.
When Eugenia sets her heart on William, Clara calls her completely irrational. "Yes," Eugenia admits, "I am mad, stark mad,
in love with him, and will be mad." Eugenia is one of Shadwell's
daring "geniuses"; she realizes instinctively William's capacity
for virtue and wedlock; to "tame so wild a man" would be a
heroine's feat. Clara's efforts to dissuade her are useless, and
they are also ironic; for, although Clara swears never to "fall in
love with a wild Fellow of the Town, if he would Jointure me
with the *East-Indies*," she not only falls in love with Wildfire,
but strains all her energy to tame and win him.

Although the girls ultimately triumph (like the women in the
comedies discussed in Chapter 4), their triumph does not,
significantly, depend upon their own courageous efforts. The
real source of their happy ending is Mr. Rant. In Act V, he
literally leads his son William out of the confusions of a dark
night and a street brawl into the light of understanding: "Into
full light, if you dare to look upon it." William's discovery that
his father was the mysterious stranger who saved him from the
law is so shocking, and Mr. Rant's impassioned sorrow is so deep,
that in the dialogues which ensue the son listens to his father
without his usual cynical banter. Rant's pleas are expressed in
blank verse, a form reserved by Restoration playwrights for
serious thought.

Rant wants William to reform, hoping to convince him of the
necessity of an ideal. William's disillusionment with ordinary
morality is no proof that it is absurd. There are commitments to
King William's commonwealth which do not permit "brutal
Fierceness that annoys/Mankind," and William is decidedly "a
Nusance to Mankind." Modestly and patriotically, Rant reminds
him that

> I gave you such an ample Income,
> 'Twould have sufficed the most extravagant,
> Except your self, and when the Court had offered
> Knighthood to me, I made it be bestowed
> On you. . . .

Such material instances of Rant's sacrifice are modified by emotionally charged moral reminders ("You have so often/Set my Eyes on flowing, that I have wondred/Whence the Moysture came that could supply them"). In a last-act reformation which we associate with some of Cibber's plays, William is instantaneously converted—"Tis the last time," "You rouse me, Sir, out of a Lethargy"—and he promises to *prove* at once the sincerity of his remarks.

When William cites the two major sources of his reformation (Rant's wisdom and Eugenia's love), he points up the ambiguous meanings of the title of the play and its central metaphor, scowrering. Wisdom and love are subtle forms of scowrering, of destroying old ways and beginning new ways: "for though you have finish'd my/Repentance, another has begun it," William tells his father. Together with Wildfire, who requires no paternal scowrering, William bows to the will of Eugenia, insisting that he has undergone a violent metamorphosis ("I am become another man"); but she, closing in on her prey, expresses again her doubts. She "must see a Sample of your New Life"; he "must be at least a years Probationer" before he can enjoy the mysteries of the conventional life he scorned.

Tope laughs at his renegade pupil. Defecting to order in the hope of achieving social-familial happiness is sheer vanity; repressing one's destructive tendencies is the surest way to folly. Tope's laughter rings out at the very moment of Rant's and Eugenia's success. William and Wildfire have assented to "the greatest Vanity on the Earth, Matrimony!" Tope is the old Pugenello whom we first met in *The Sullen Lovers*—more mellow perhaps, more laughable than terrifying. He will carry on the devilish tradition of scowrering with his new pupils, Whackum and the Alsatians, but clearly these dull youths promise a decline in the Art of Destruction.

II *The Enemy at Home and Abroad*

The Volunteers may be regarded as a companion piece to *The Scowrers* because it also is concerned with those familial-emotional powers which can direct youth's great energy to man's good.[4] *The Volunteers* is about soldiers, and its recurrent metaphors are military ones which stress the idea that lovers, like warriors, must surrender to forces more powerful than themselves. Neither Young Hackwell, the hero, nor his companion, Welford, has a taste for rakish life. They do not idly vent their power on a war at home against English citizens; from the beginning of the play, we see that they are dutiful servants of the state, offering their power and their lives to King William in his righteous crusades against Catholic France. Indeed, this play, it seems to me, is a tribute to the English monarchy more valid and impressive than Shadwell's laureate effusions, for William and Mary are implicitly designated in the play as the prototypes of the new kind of hero and heroine. Like them, Hackwell and his Eugenia are serious people, abjuring folly; they are respecters of authority, conscious of the differences between truth and falsehood, sentimental to a degree, shy perhaps, and (as far as the comic mode will allow them to be) heroic.

The educational motive is apparent in the contrasts and comparisons between young fools and young wisemen, old fools and old wisemen—between the two fathers of the play and their offspring, and between the relative confusion or stability of the fathers' households. The good educator is Major General Blunt, a Cavalier during the Puritan Revolution, "somewhat rough in his Speech, but very brave and honest, and of good Understanding, and a good Patriot," according to the description in the Dramatis Personae. A country man, he has come to London to marry off his daughters, clever Eugenia and vacuous Teresia, a girl charmed by frivolity, fashion, and the arch-fop of Shadwell's comedies, Sir Nicholas Dainty. The relationship between Blunt and his daughters is subtle and ironic. Eugenia shares his honesty, but not his gross candidness. Teresia shares his candidness, but not his common sense. Her *grand amour* Sir Nicholas, unlike Hackwell and Welford, is a comic soldier, all "form" without substance. He changes his beau's costume for a uniform, and he volunteers to join the armies abroad because soldiering is the latest fashion. So also Hop, a dancing master, knows all the formal movements of the latest dances and presents a delicate, fine outward show; but, a cardboard man, he lacks the firm heroic mettle to make him a hero.

Blunt dominates the play as a master of ceremonies who brings together all the young lovers and demands that they reveal their true emotions. If such strategy fails, as in the case of Dainty and

Teresia, he forces the beau to take her, lest her madcap lust for him lose her her maidenhead. In his crude way, Blunt protects his *infants* and directs his world so that the forces of love and desire are satisfied. To his house he invites a number of characters, and the house assumes a symbolic significance. It is the place where masks are dropped and truths expressed.

Among the guests are his old Cavalier friends, officers who do nothing but get drunk and relive the battles they fought. They dwell pathetically on the past, while Blunt is concerned about the future and his daughters' happiness. He admires his friends, but he sees in the modern age of William and Mary a more sober greatness than the somewhat frivolous greatness of Cavalier England. He is closer to Hackwell and Welford, the new breed and hope of the nation; they are not boisterous but downright committed men. Hackwell is a professional soldier; Welford is a volunteer who has, with his own funds, furnished men and arms to assist King William abroad.

The patriotic, serious attitude of this new breed informs the general attitudes toward action and love in the play. Young Hackwell is a member of the "other" house, his father's house where nothing of Blunt's geniality prevails. At Colonel Hackwell's deception abounds, for it is a kingdom with a puppet monarch. The Colonel is "an old Anabaptist . . . of *Cromwell's*" who fought against the crown, as he ambiguously puts it, "on Principle"—that is, for money as well as for ideals. The satire on Puritanism, typically Shadwellian, plays upon the habit of the Puritan mind to link spiritualism and moneymaking without, however, understanding the true value of religion and of financial power.

Colonel Hackwell relives the past nostalgically, like his old enemies, the Cavaliers. He never criticizes the new monarchs, but neither does he feel strong patriotic sentiments. Indeed, he reaps a benefit from the wars as a stockjobber. His view of life is narrow: he is blind to the most obvious virtues and vices existing in his house, the atmosphere of which is utterly oppressive to his son and his daughter Clara, whom Welford loves. His children cannot impress him with their virtues, for he is dominated by a young wife who is in the process of disinheriting the Hackwell children by scandalizing them. Assisted by her cowardly paramour Nickum, she wants to make herself and her clownish daughter Winifred the Colonel's heirs. Before the comedy opens, she has already managed to drive the son from the house; and, by Act IV, Clara also leaves, following her brother to the sanctuary of Blunt's establishment. The Colonel's house is a center of disorder, vulgarity, criminality; good people fly from it to find protection and understanding at Blunt's.

The distinction between the houses and their owners is proliferated and modified as the action progresses, and it is directly related to the central metaphors of volunteering and of war. Of her own free will, Clara volunteers to join the Blunts. With some brief persuasion by Blunt, Clara and Eugenia marry Hackwell and Welford, respectively; and these men, already willing soldiers of the King, volunteer to commit themselves to wedlock. The characters who thus willingly act exhibit the finest capacity for heroism—military and domestic.

This will to do is the key to the meaning of *The Volunteers*. It is emphasized, by contrast, in the characters who have little will—who are driven by their "humors." Fashion drives Sir Nicholas to join the army and Blunt makes him wed Teresia. Old Hackwell renounces his wife only after many emphatic expositions of her adultery. Even certain minor figures (Tim Kastril and Winifred) achieve a degree of happiness in their indefatigable urge to be what they desire. Cowardly Kastril, attempting unsuccessfully to compete with Sir Nicholas as a beau-about-town, is accidentally drawn into a duel with the bully Nickum. Kastril soon learns that courage is easy (when one fights with a coward who runs) and so he becomes a braggart warrior. Featherbrained Winifred accomplishes her purpose in wedding the dancing master Hop, her ideal man, but the triumph is comic, a projection of her own shallow ideals. These low comic denouements mirror in shallow or silly ways those of the high plot. The ultimate distinctions between high and low plots are distinctions between ways of volunteering: the will which drives some to a meaningful joy differs from that which drives others to meaningless joy, sufficient for fools.

The war metaphor is sustained in the London setting. Far from the battlefields of France occur various wars and rebellions, domestic and amorous. They duplicate, often ironically, English wars and rebellions of the past and the present. Old military victories and defeats, the styles of Cavalier and Roundhead, are contained within the context of Blunt's house. And though long retired from war, Blunt carries on his part as a strategist. He implicitly regards it as his patriotic duty to see that young people channel their powers for the specific good of England and, ultimately, for the good of civilization. There are the usual romantic barriers between the worthy people: Eugenia and Clara are too modest to pursue their heroes, for example.

But there is a concern, new in Shadwell's comedies, which stops the girls from submitting easily to marriage: they seriously fear being widowed by the war. Hackwell declares that honor is an absolute concomitant to love in Act III: "I value your Favour so vastly . . . , that I would quit for you my Country, and my chase of Fame; but that I know you would despise me for't." The patriotic Eugenia agrees but insists that "Love-Treaties shou'd be Adjourn'd till softer times of Peace," for she is unable "to set my heart upon one who may be lost in every Rencounter or Attaque." Although her arguments are in part typical maneuvers to sustain her inaccessibility, she is also in greater part telling the truth. Hackwell's answer to her fears points to the larger significance of their relationship by introducing the images of William and Mary as exemplary people:

> *Hackwell junior.* Does not our Royal Mistress do the same and bears it with a Princely Magnanimity; She and our Country have the greatest Stake in *Europe,* who will be sure to hazard himself with the bravest.
> *Eugenia.* She is to be reverenc'd and admir'd, but hard it is to Imitate so Glorious an Example; and methinks a private Lady may be happier.
> *Hackwell junior.* We cannot in Gratitude pretend to be happier, than those from whom we have our Happiness; in them our Countreys Cause, and yours, and all's at stake.

Blunt, however, brings them together. He reveals the secret passion of Eugenia and Clara, ranting against "damn'd Raptures and senseless Romantick stuff" of courtship, insisting that the lovers "Never use more words than need." A military man, he calls for immediate action; and his unromantic directness is a source of the good-natured humor of the play, particularly as it undercuts the delicate intricacies of the verbal love battles. War demands its heroic girls as well as its heroes; private happiness is not all that matters; the future waits for Eugenia's assent, for through her and men like Hackwell, the continuity of a hearty English race is assured. If she postpones the wedding, she is an "Ass of a Daughter!" and will be "like a Fellow whose Bridge was a falling,—Would not flux because times were unsettled: Does not War make a Destruction of Men? What should good Subjects do then;—But lay about them to replenish. A dod, this young Fellow and his Friend, are gallant Fellows! And if they be knockt o'the head this Summer,—I'd have some of the breed left,—which is almost lost in *England*." We have come a long way from the crabbedness of Goldingham in this plain-dealing old man who, perhaps like Shadwell himself in his last years, did not allow the trials of his life to wither his belief that comic triumphs were possible. Blunt applies his *carpe diem* theme to a wartime world and, in the ambiguous *good Subjects,* to the comic mode. Good subjects, whether in a political or a dramatic context, are necessary if the nation and the theater are to survive successfully.

Blunt has no messages for the marrying fools of the play. They will thrive and replenish—in Blunt's world, in England, or in the world of comedy—no matter what one does. But the wise and witty will heed the lesson which can bring them the best hope for personal and public happiness in an uncertain life, the best hope for present and future possibilities. This was, in effect, the great outcome of Shadwell's comedies, from *The Sullen Lovers* to this last, more mellow satire.

CHAPTER 9

Shadwell and Restoration Drama

IN recent years critics have remarked the quantity of confusion and misdirection which informs the body of nineteenth-century and early twentieth-century criticism of Restoration drama. It is beyond the scope of this study to consider the critical problems involved in defining Restoration comedy, problems which have been thoroughly revaluated by writers like Fujimura, Underwood, and Holland, but it is important to observe that these revaluations do not take Shadwell explicitly into account. Up to this time, his place not only has been not clearly ascertained but has been a matter of uncertainty. But no longer, I believe, can we assume that our idea of Restoration achievement in drama is adequate if we overlook Shadwell. That he was esteemed by an age whose tastes and interest in drama were highly sensitive and sharply defined should in itself alert us to his importance.

In the opening lines of his influential *The Comedy of Manners*, John Palmer, attempting to narrow his study to four or five major writers, voiced his uncertainty regarding Shadwell: "Who are the comic dramatists of the Restoration? Dryden [Sedley, Buckingham, Rochester, Behn, Crowne, Settle, and Cibber] wrote comedies; Shadwell's *Squire of Alsatia* was as popular in its day and regarded as of equal importance with *The Country Wife*." But Palmer, following Hunt, Macaulay, and Hazlitt, decided that there "are four undoubtedly great figures in our comic literature between Shakespeare and Sheridan," and that, except for one more, Etherege, "Further selection is difficult." He eliminated Shadwell, apparently sixth in line, although with hesitation: "If we admit Etherege, should we not also admit Shadwell . . . ?" But Palmer was interested in "the origins and development of the English Comedy of Manners," and he thought of Shadwell as "unnecessary" to the "Main course of this development."[1] Other critics have similarly relegated Shadwell to a minor position, but often with a word of warning that he is more impressive than is generally believed to be the case by those who have not read him, or by those who have read him cursorily, or by those who have read him primarily to compare him to the major writers of Restoration comedy.

There is no need to disagree with Palmer that Shadwell was not in the main course of the comedy of manners which he discusses, but there is a need to counter the general tendency to think of Shadwell specifically *in* that course, but as a minor figure in it. Reappraisals of his contribution depend initially on how we define the comedy of manners or wit, on how flexible a definition we are willing to make, and on how readily we would include in it Shadwell's harsh, uncompromising satiric view of humanity which, in certain stylistic and moralizing ways, is close to Wycherley's *Plain Dealer* and anticipates Swift's satires. The broadest and fairest definition would have to include his kind of comedy, if only because it exists as a firm part of Restoration dramatic expression. Definitive considerations of Restoration drama would be faulty, then, if Shadwell's place in it is not understood.

This is not to say that his plays, particularly his comedies, do not reflect many conventional Restoration techniques and themes. As I have shown, he is, in most ways, of his age—not a distinctive offshoot. In a sense, more fluently than many of his contemporaries, Shadwell responds to and depicts the Restoration world picture. Irony permeates his plays; man in society is its locus; wit and wisdom are its ideals. But his concern for characterization, as intense though not so brilliantly realized as Congreve's, sets him apart in many ways. His successful adaptation of the older Jonsonian "humors" principles for an age so uncertain about human greatness, makes him a traditionalist who transmutes the tradition by his freshness of approach, by his ability to move rapidly from one comic crisis to another, and by that sustained sense of comedy as ritual in which playgoers may, for three hours or so, enter into his world and sense clearly and sardonically the satiric conditions of their universe. We must guard against misleading comparisons of Shadwell to the high comic dramatists of the age. One recent critic who regards the "comic verve" of *The Libertine* as an indication of Shadwell's comic power suffused in a tragic mode, is already "persuaded that a stage which welcomes Ionesco is once more ready for Shadwell's bizarre comedy," which he does "not hesitate to call one of the most impressive plays of its epoch."[2] I believe that we can call most of Shadwell's plays impressive and that it would not be in the least misleading, in venturing a twentieth-century context, to say that Shadwell's line emerges not in the high sophistications of Philip Barry or of Noel Coward, but in the earthy *bizarreries* of Giraudoux, Beckett, Pinter, and Albee and in the farcical cynicisms of the Marx Brothers or W. C. Fields.

Notes and References

To avoid encumbering this study with numerous footnotes and references, I do not cite specific acts or page numbers when I refer to passages and scenes from Shadwell's works. From the context of my discussions, the reader may easily locate the passages and scenes, all references to which are from Montague Summers' five volume edition, *The Works of Thomas Shadwell* (London, 1927). The contents of each volume and the inclusive pages are as follows: I. *The Sullen Lovers* (7-92), *The Royal Shepherdess* (99-173), *The Humorists* (181-255); II. *The Miser* (15-93), *Epsom-Wells* (101-82), *The Tempest* (193-269), *Psyche* (277-340); III. *The Libertine* (19-93), *The Virtuoso* (101-82), *Timon of Athens* (193-275), *A True Widow* (283-363); IV. *The Woman-Captain* (13-85), *The Lancashire Witches* (99-189), *The Squire of Alsatia* (201-83), *Bury-Fair* (293-369); V. *The Amorous Bigotte* (13-78), *The Scowrers* (85-150), *The Volunteers* (157-224), and poems, essays, and letters (227-404).

Chapter One

1. For most of the biographical material, I am indebted to the only two full-length studies of Shadwell: Albert S. Borgman, *Thomas Shadwell: His Life and Comedies* (New York, 1928), and Montague Summers' Introduction, *The Works*, I, xvii-ccli. D. M. Walmsley's Biography in his edition of *Epsom Wells and The Volunteers or The Stock-Jobbers* (Boston, 1930), pp. vii-xvii, corrects some of the material in Borgman and Summers. These writers base their information on "Some Account of the Author and his Writings," prefixed to the four volume *The Dramatick Works of Thomas Shadwell, Esq.* (London, 1720), which includes a dedication to George I signed by Thomas' son, Sir John. Shadwell occasionally alluded to his life in prefaces and dedications; the most informative piece is the Dedication of *The Tenth Satyr of Juvenal*, in which he defended himself against some of Dryden's personal attacks.

2. See Dedication, *Epsom-Wells*. A sketch of the Shadwell-Newcastle relationship appears in Henry Ten Eyck Perry, *The First Duchess of Newcastle and Her Husband as Figures in Literary History* (Boston, 1918), pp. 155-56, especially.

3. Four plays were dedicated to Newcastle (*The Sullen Lovers, Epsom-Wells, The Libertine, The Virtuoso*); one to his wife (*The Humorists*); one to his grandson, Lord Henry Ogle (*The Woman-Captain*). Among other important patrons to whom the plays were dedicated are Buckingham (*Timon of Athens*); Dorset (*The Miser, The Squire of Alsatia, Bury-Fair*); Monmouth (*Psyche*); Sedley (*A True Widow*).

4. For an account of Mrs. Shadwell, see John Harold Wilson, *All the King's Ladies: Actresses of the Restoration* (Chicago, 1958), pp. 186-87, especially.

5. For remarks on Dryden and on Shadwell's dramatic silence, see below, p. 179, n. 5.

6. *The Medal of John Bayes* was published in May, 1682, and *Mac Flecknoe* in October of the same year. As much research has shown, Dryden's poem was written earlier and, according to recent findings by J. M. Osborn and David Vieth, may have been circulated in manuscript *before* 1678; see George deF. Lord, ed., *Poems on Affairs of State: Augustan Satirical Verse, 1660-1714* (New Haven, 1963), I, 376. No doubt, Shadwell knew of Dryden's poem, and his satire was, in good part, a retaliation. Citations from *Mac Flecknoe* in this study are from Lord, I, 378-86.

7. Dryden in *Mac Flecknoe* and Settle in the Preface to *Ibrahim* (1677) refer to *The Hypocrite*, an unpublished comedy by Shadwell, probably acted in 1670 or 1671. Shadwell may also have assisted Newcastle in preparing for the stage, in 1674, *The Triumphant Widow, or The Medley of Humours*. For remarks on this play in relation to *Bury-Fair*, see Perry, pp. 157-65.

8. David H. Stevens, ed., *Types of English Drama, 1660-1780* (Boston, 1923), p. 886. *Bury-Fair* is reprinted in this anthology.

9. Brady's sermon is in Summers, I, cclix-cclxiv, and letters by Shadwell on Brady's play in V, 403, 404, and in Brice Harris, *Charles Sackville, Sixth Earl of Dorset, Patron and Poet of the Restoration* (Urbana, 1940), p. 158.

10. See *Letters upon Several Occasions* (London, 1696), p. 129.

11. For brief discussions of Shadwell's achievement, see, among many others, Adolphus William Ward, *A History of English Dramatic Literature to the Death of Queen Anne* (London, 1899), III, 455-61; and Allardyce Nicoll, *A History of English Drama, 1660-1900*, 4th ed. (Cambridge, 1955), I, 201-10, 429-31, especially.

12. *The History of Witchcraft and Demonology* (New York, 1956), p. 297.

13. Sir Walter Scott and George Saintsbury, eds., *The Works of John Dryden* (Edinburgh, 1885), X, 439 n.

14. Sybil Rosenfeld, ed., *The Letterbook of Sir George Etherege*

(London, 1928), p. 338. See also, p. 421. Rochester and Langbaine were among many other seventeenth-century admirers of Shadwell.

15. See Borgman, pp. 113-14. Scott's works include *The Fortunes of Nigel* and *Peveril of the Peak.*

16. Dougald MacMillan and Howard Mumford Jones, eds., *Plays of the Restoration and Eighteenth Century* (New York, 1931), p. 258.

17. *Thomas Shadwell,* p. 5.

18. In a perceptive article by Thomas B. Stroup, "Shadwell's Use of Hobbes," *Studies in Philology,* XXXV (1938), 405-32, the influence of the author of *The Leviathan* is traced in several of Shadwell's works with special focus on such themes as atheism, epicureanism, and the problem of free will. Stroup rightly stresses the use of the word *will* in the definition of "humors," since it is the word which distinguishes this definition from Jonson's; and he sees a firm connection between the theory and Hobbist determinism. However, it should be noted that, for Shadwell, man unwisely *chose* to stick by a ruling passion and was ultimately trapped by it.

19. Preface (*An Evening's Love,* 1671), *Essays of John Dryden,* ed., W. P. Ker (Oxford, 1900), I, 135-36. The Dryden-Shadwell controversies have been a favorite subject for critics. In "Shadwell's Impact Upon John Dryden," *Review of English Studies,* XX (1944), 29-44, R. Jack Smith demonstrates the seriousness with which both disputants approached their esthetic differences. As he, and Walmsley, pp. xxix-xli, suggest, it is a mistake to regard Shadwell as an inferior critic. Cf. Frank Harper Moore, *The Nobler Pleasure: Dryden's Comedy in Theory and Practice* (Chapel Hill, 1963), pp. 85 ff., where, more conventionally, Shadwell's adulation of Jonson is considered primarily a part of his effort to win and keep Newcastle's favor.

20. John Harrington Smith, *The Gay Couple in Restoration Comedy* (Cambridge, Mass., 1948), pp. 120, 124. But Smith stresses the moralizing influence, especially after *A True Widow,* by Shadwell's insistence on virtuous couples; see also, "Shadwell, the Ladies, and the Change in Comedy," *Modern Philology,* XLVI (1948), 22-33. Yet Shadwell dealt ironically with virtuous characters, even in the late, more explicitly moral, comedies. According to Ernest Bernbaum, elements in a comedy like *The Squire of Alsatia,* "which appear to approach sentimental comedy, are really illustrations of the flexibility of the prevailing [witty or satiric] comic methods," *The Drama of Sensibility: A Sketch of the History of English Sentimental Comedy and Domestic Tragedy, 1696-1780* (Cambridge, Mass., 1925), p. 69. But consider my remarks below, pp. 146, 158, 162.

21. In the Preface to *An Evening's Love,* Dryden talks of a "mixed way of Comedy; that which is neither all wit, nor all humour, but the

result of both," *Essays*, I, 139. Although this kind of comedy seems close to Shadwell's manner of blending witty and humorous materials, Dryden's further comments on the kind cannot be applied to Shadwell.

22. *The Restoration Comedy of Wit* (Princeton, 1952), pp. 13-15, and elsewhere.

23. Elisabeth Mignon calls Shadwell's portraits of old people the most brutal in a comic tradition sharply defined by Etherege, Wycherley, and Shadwell, in *Crabbed Age and Youth: The Old Men and Women in the Restoration Comedy of Manners* (Durham, 1947), pp. 73-82. It is usually against such superannuated persons that the young girls in the plays revolt. In his later plays, Shadwell tended to idealize some of his old men.

24. Dale Underwood, *Etherege and the Seventeenth-Century Comedy of Manners* (New Haven, 1957), pp. 61, 71, 91-93, and elsewhere.

25. Preface (*An Evening's Love*), *Essays*, I, 137.

Chapter Two

1. The success of the *Lovers* is often attributed to the caricaturing of Sir Robert Howard (Sir Positive); Edward Howard (Ninny); Susan Uphill, Sir Robert's mistress (Lady Vaine); and Oliver St. John (Woodcock). See Pepys's remarks, *The Diary of Samuel Pepys*, ed. Henry B. Wheatley (London, 1924), entries for May 2, 4, 5, 8, and June 24, 1668; and April 14, 1669. See also, Montague Summers, *The Playhouse of Pepys* (London, 1935), pp. 167, 180. *The Humorists* was poorly received. According to Shadwell's Preface, it "came upon the Stage with all the disadvantages imaginable"—among them, the excision of objectionable portions, antagonists in the audience, and actors unfamiliar with their parts. After the second day, however, "excellent *Dancings*" were added; then the play was moderately successful.

2. Molière's influence on Shadwell has long been the subject of study. Sometimes Shadwell cited his borrowings; usually he did not. On the subject, see among others, Dudley Howe Miles, *The Influence of Molière on Restoration Comedy* (New York, 1910); and John Wilcox, *The Relation of Molière to Restoration Comedy* (New York, 1938). It seems to me that consideration of the specific adaptations (*Miser, Psyche*) is most fruitful.

3. "Introduction," *Thomas Shadwell* (London, n. d.), p. 3. Shadwell's defense of the "design" seems to be directed against current objections.

4. Save in a few instances, Shadwell utilizes opening scenes to set forth the crucial thematic-philosophic attitudes of his plays.

5. The best seventeenth-century discussion of Juvenal and Horace is Dryden's *A Discourse Concerning the Original and Progress of Satire* (1693), *Essays*, II, 26 ff. Consult also Alvin B. Kernan, *The Cankered Muse: Satire of the English Renaissance* (New Haven, 1959), pp. 64 ff.

6. The idea of "uncertainty" as a dominant motive in Restoration comedy is excellently discussed in Norman N. Holland, *The First Modern Comedies: The Significance of Etherege, Wycherley and Congreve* (Cambridge, Mass., 1959), pp. 271, 220, 224, and elsewhere.

7. See Enid Welsford, *The Fool: His Social and Literary History* (Garden City, 1961), pp. 304 ff. According to remarks made in Act I of *The Woman-Captain*, Shadwell may have regarded "humors" characters as modern instances of the Renaissance fool.

8. See Northrop Frye, *Anatomy of Criticism: Four Essays* (Princeton, 1957), pp. 164 ff.

9. Shadwell would have called Crazy's sexual desire an unlikely subject for comedy; his *excessive* lust makes him a "humors" character.

10. Kathleen M. Lynch, *The Social Mode of Restoration Comedy* (New York, 1926), p. 159. An illuminating analysis of *L'Avare,* which should be considered in conjunction with my reading of *The Miser,* appears in J. D. Hubert, *Molière and the Comedy of Intellect* (Berkeley, 1962), pp. 204-17.

11. Shadwell's important additional characters are Tim Squeeze; the prostitutes—Lettice, Joyce, and Bridget; the gamblers—Rant and Hazard.

Chapter Three

1. See Borgman, p. 153, and Nicoll, who thinks of *Epsom* as a comedy of manners, p. 205. Lynch believes that *She Wou'd* set the pattern for all of Shadwell's comedies; she considers Shadwell the chief link between Etherege and Congreve, for "between the completion of Etherege's work and the beginning of Congreve's," Shadwell was "the only dramatist of any distinction at all who attempted to save for true comedy an age which was . . . running mad after farces. From Shadwell alone of the comic dramatists whose plays mark these seventeen years, Congreve, from time to time, made noteworthy borrowings," p. 182.

2. *Diary,* entry for July 26, 1663, and elswhere.

3. "Of English Comedy," *The Works of Monsieur de St. Évremond, Made from the French Original: with the Life of the Author; by Mr. Des Maiseaux,* 2nd ed. (London, 1728), II, 171.

4. When citing dialogue, I give the full names of characters, here and elsewhere. For example, *Bevil* appears as *Bev.* in Shadwell.

5. The importance of Lucretius and of Epicureanism in Restoration thought, particularly as a background to the drama, is discussed by Underwood, pp. 10-40.

6. See Claude Lloyd, "Shadwell and the Virtuosi," *PMLA,* XLIV (1929), 472-94.

7. Borgman discusses these sources (pp. 168-73), and others have added to his findings. According to Everett L. Jones, "Robert Hooke and *The Virtuoso,*" *Modern Language Notes,* LXVI (1951), 180-82, Hooke regarded the play as a personal attack. Although Shadwell ridicules certain experimental aspects of the Royal Society, he also seconds its disapproval of florid expression in the caricature of Sir Formal Trifle, who is not a scientist.

8. G. Blakemore Evans, "The Sources of Shadwell's Character of Sir Formal Trifle in 'The Virtuoso'," *Modern Language Review,* XXXV (1940), 211-14. Evans traces Sir Formal to Davenant's Sir Solemn Trifle in *News from Plymouth,* a pre-Commonwealth play first published in 1673. Florence R. Scott disagrees with Evans that Sir Solemn may have been the model for Shadwell's first pompous "humor," in " 'News from Plimouth' and Sir Positive At-All," *Modern Language Review,* XXXIX (1944), 183-85. I suggest that Sir Humphrey (*Scowrers*) also resembles Sir Solemn, but see below, my reference to Jonson, p. 160.

9. In Dryden, Richard Flecknoe replaces Sir Formal as the dupe: "For Bruce and Longvil had a trap prepar'd,/And down they sent the yet declaiming bard" (ll. 212-13).

Chapter Four

1. In the Dedication to Sedley, Shadwell thanked him for having *"review'd all my Plays, as they came incorrectly and in hast from my hands"*—a remark which may have served as ammunition for *Mac Flecknoe,* ll. 163-64. Since Shadwell *is* witty and since the extent of Sedley's assistance cannot be determined, it is difficult to agree with Vivian de Sola Pinto that "flashes of wit that lighten up the scenes of some of his best comedies are, no doubt, often due to the Baronet's pen," *Sir Charles Sedley, 1639-1701: A Study in the Life and Literature of the Restoration* (London, 1927), p. 108, and n. 2 in which some evidence is given. Pinto describes the close relationship between patron and playwright, including the fact that Shadwell named him a trustee for his widow, pp. 107-8, 168 ff., 209. In the Dedication, Shadwell lavishly praises Sedley's *Antony and Cleopatra* (produced in 1677, a year after Dryden's *All for Love*), with the

implication that his rival's tragedy was far inferior. No doubt, his comments contributed to the Dryden-Shadwell feuds of the late 1670's and 1680's.

2. For a good discussion of the playhouse scene as a "realistic" reproduction of Restoration playgoing, see Dale Farnsworth Smith, *Plays About the Theatre in England* (London, 1936), pp. 52-56.

3. The Mrs. Gripe plot is based upon Montfluery's *La Fille Captaine;* see John Harrington Smith, "French Sources for Six English Comedies, 1660-1750," *Journal of English and Germanic Philology,* XLVII (1948), 390. Characteristically, Shadwell exaggerates the English heroine's aggressive tendencies.

4. His religious satire, which caused a furor before the play was acted, had to be excised, and he was *"forced, in my own Vindication, to Print the whole Play just as I writ it"* ("To the Reader"). Stroup, who discusses the Hobbist-Deist thought, regards the play as a satire on supernaturalism, pp. 423-25. But he overlooks the ironic fact that witches *exist* in Shadwell's Lancashire. Regarding witchcraft, Shadwell said that he was *"costive of belief."* Elaborate notes for Acts I, II, III and V, show his abundant knowledge of the black art. Summers contends that most of his information comes secondhand from Reginald Scott's *Discoverie of Witchcraft* (*Works,* IV, 89): Borgman, citing other sources, compares the masque scenes to Jonson's *Masque of Queens,* upon which Shadwell heavily relied, pp. 193-98. See also Summers, *Witchcraft and Demonology,* pp. 276-313.

5. In "To the Reader," Kelly-Tegue is called *"one of the Murderers of Sir* Edmond-Bury Godfrey." The extent of Shadwell's connection with the Whigs at this time is not clear. At the time of his marriage, he may have been a Catholic, but most of his associates after the *Witches* were Whigs. His commitment to William and Mary and his adherence to the principles of the Revolution are unquestionable.

Chapter Five

1. Jeannette Marks, *English Pastoral Drama, From the Restoration to the Date of the Publication of the "Lyrical Ballads"* (1660-1798), (London, 1908), p. 56. Fountain's play is briefly treated by Alfred Harbage, *Cavalier Drama, An Historical and Critical Supplement to the Study of the Elizabethan and Restoration Stages* (New York, 1936), p. 221. Stroup (pp. 413-22) considers the plays analyzed in this chapter the best sources for Shadwell's Hobbist attitudes.

2. See especially, Hazelton Spencer, *Shakespeare Improved: The Restoration Versions in Quarto and on the Stage* (Cambridge, Mass., 1927), pp. 192-210. Argument has raged as to Shadwell's contribu-

tion to the operatic version; a fine summary of major attitudes, with
the conclusion that Shadwell is probably responsible for the opera,
appears in William A. Milton, *"Tempest* in a Teapot," *Journal of
English Literary History,* XIV (1947), 207-18. Consult also, James G.
McManaway, "Songs and Masques in *The Tempest,*" *Luttrell Society
Reprints,* No. 14 (1953), 71-96. Ever since Congreve's 1717 edition
of Dryden, Shadwell's version has been reprinted in Dryden's col-
lected plays. The original Dryden-Davenant version is available in
*Shakespeare Adaptations: The Tempest, The Mock Tempest, and
King Lear,* ed. Montague Summers (Boston, 1922).

   3. *Shakespeare Improved,* p. 203.

   4. *Works of John Dryden,* I, 91.

   5. Oscar Mandel, in *The Theatre of Don Juan: A Collection of
Plays and Views, 1630-1963* (Lincoln, 1963), reprints *The Libertine,*
often considered a "locus of libertinism" in Restoration drama. He
compares it to recent treatments of "Absurd Man" such as Jarry's
Ubu Roi and Camus' *The Stranger* because it is "consciously the
enactment of a philosophical doctrine" and because "it makes explicit
the systematic hedonism" of Restoration comedy. See pp. 164-69.
Mandel also discusses Rosimond's play which is collected in *Les
Contemporaines de Molière,* ed. V. Fournel (Paris, 1875), III, 313-77.

   6. *Shakespeare Improved,* p. 286. He considered *The Tempest*
the worst. See pp. 281-87, for an outline and discussion of Shadwell's *Timon.*

   7. H. J. Oliver, ed., *Timon of Athens* (London, 1959), p. 152.

   8. *Shakespeare Improved,* p. 287.

Chapter Six

   1. *Poetry and Politics Under the Stuarts* (Cambridge, 1960), pp.
201-3. Two of the most recent books which briefly discuss Shadwell's poems are Edmund K. Broadus, *The Laureateship: A Study of
the Office of Poet Laureate in England with Some Account of the
Poets* (Oxford, 1921), pp. 74-88; and Kenneth Hopkins, *The Poets
Laureate* (New York, 1955), pp. 32-43, 205-7.

   2. The problem of reading songs, prologues, and epilogues in and
out of context has often troubled critics. As a background to the
problem, see William R. Bowden, *The English Dramatic Lyric, 1603-
1642: A Study in Stuart Dramatic Technique* (New Haven, 1951),
pp. 79-86, particularly; and Arthur W. Hoffman, *John Dryden's
Imagery* (Gainesville, 1962), pp. 20-22.

   3. Among the other satires sometimes attributed to Shadwell and
printed in Summers are *Satyr to His Muse* (1682), *The Tory-Poets:*

A Satyr (1683), and *The Address of John Dryden, Laureat to His Highness the Prince of Orange* (1689). Major bibliographical problems concerning some of these poems are presented by George R. Noyes, ed., *The Poetical Works of Dryden* (Boston, 1950), pp. xlv-xlviii. See also, D. M. McKeithan, "The Authorship of *The Medal of John Bayes*," *University of Texas Studies in English*, No. 12 (1932), pp. 92-97.

4. The *Ode for Queen Mary's Birthday* (1691), printed in Summers, is "probably but not certainly by Shadwell," according to Broadus, p. 80.

5. Three of Shadwell's pieces were written for occasions other than the production of his own plays: Epilogue (Laurence Maidwell's *The Loving Enemies*, 1682), Epilogue (Nicholas Brady's *The Rape*, 1691/2), and "A Lenten Prologue Refus'd by the Players" (1682), reprinted in Autrey Nell Wiley, *Rare Prologues and Epilogues, 1642-1700* (London, 1940), pp. 161-63. This last Prologue was "refus'd" apparently for its Whiggish sentiments. Wiley cites a passage from *The Muses Mercury* (1707) which suggests the kind of opposition Shadwell faced in having his plays produced after 1681; according to the passage, Shadwell said that *"while Mr. Dryden was Poet Laureat, he wou'd never let any Play of his be Acted,"* and Shadwell retaliated in 1690 by preventing Dryden's Prologue to *The Prophetess* from being spoken after the opening night.

6. Among his snatches and refrains are lines from the song in *The Miser* (*"Diseases and Troubles are ne'r to be found"*), a subtle echo of the ideas which I have discussed above, pp. 123-24.

7. See his detailed notes to *Tenth Satyr*.

8. Of the poems which can safely be attributed to Shadwell, two celebrate the monarchs' arrival; three, their birthdays; and two, William's Irish wars.

Chapter Seven

1. Both comedies were dedicated to the Earl of Dorset who secured the laureateship for Shadwell. Act I of *The Squire* was written at Copt-Hall (or Copped Hall), Dorset's country estate. In the Dedication, there is a faint hint of a parallel between Ned Belfond (who retires from the anxieties of libertine restlessness) and Dorset (who, with a fine wife, removes himself far from *"all the unsatisfying pleasures, and noisie troubles of the Town to so sweet a place . . ."*). In the Dedication of *Bury*, Shadwell warmly thanks Dorset for the laureateship, speaks of his illness, and defends the Revolution in terms which clearly echo his recurrent comic theme: the conflict between paternal tyrants and youthful rebels. William and

Mary are the benevolent paternal figures. In his late plays, except for *The Amorous Bigotte,* Shadwell creates admirable paternal figures.

2. The importance of Terence's comedy in Augustan drama is discussed by Bernbaum, pp. 16-26.

3. In the Dedication, Shadwell discusses the matter of disobedience to monarchs and regards the rejection of James II by the English people as a modern instance of the disobedience in Genesis. But he goes on to distinguish between religious and legal (or political) obedience in the Lockean manner which is also apparent in his apologies for the Glorious Revolution in his official verse.

4. Summers, *Works,* pp. cci-cciv, provides a long excerpt from a discussion of *The Squire* by Thomas Cook ("Considerations on the Stage, etc.," published in 1731), in which the moral lessons of Ned's reform are stressed. See also, a general discussion of the reforming hero in David S. Berkeley, "The Penitent Rake in Restoration Comedy," *Modern Philology,* XLIX (1952), 223-33, where *The Scowrers* is briefly mentioned.

5. Jean Elizabeth Gagen, *The New Woman: Her Emergence in English Drama, 1660-1730* (New York, 1954), pp. 48-50.

Chapter Eight

1. Although Borgman considers the sequel "a decidedly inferior piece," I find it a striking attempt to speed up incidents at so rapid a rate that the farcical tempo reduces all the action to a kind of kinetic absurdity. The atmosphere of Spain is as "madly comic," as intentionally absurd in this play, as it was "madly tragic" in *The Libertine.* According to the Prologue, Shadwell associated these two plays, both of which are set in Spain.

2. *John Gay's London: Illustrated from the Poetry of the Time* (Cambridge, Mass., 1928), p. 247.

3. For a fine analysis of the Park symbol as Wycherley employs it, see Holland, pp. 42-43.

4. Walmsley remarks, "The subsidiary theme of the stockjobbers, which shows very little connection with the main plot, is so slight as scarcely to warrant the subtitle of the play," p. 204. And elsewhere, citing from the *Dictionary of the Canting Crew* (c. 1720), he defines stockjobbing as "a sharp, cunning, cheating Trade of Buying and Selling Shares of Stock in East-India, Guinea and other Companies; also in the Bank, Exchequer etc.," p. 365. Certainly, however, this cheating, in which old Hackwell is the major culprit, is directly related to the question of patriotism, of *giving* to the nation rather than selfishly of taking from it. I suggest, moreover, that

Shadwell intended to elaborate more fully on the contrast between *stockjobbing* and *volunteering* but that death prevented him from doing so.

Chapter Nine

1. (London, 1913), pp. 2-3.
2. Oscar Mandel, in his assessment of plays dealing with Don Juan, p. 169. See also, above, p. 178, n. 5.

Selected Bibliography

PRIMARY SOURCES

Omitted from this chronological listing are his minor poems and re-printings of his plays in college anthologies, for some of which, see pp. 244, n. 8; 245, n. 16. Dates of other reprintings, appearing in brackets, are given for the plays.

The Sullen Lovers: or, The Impertinents. London: Henry Herringman, 1668. [1670, 1693.]

The Royal Shepherdess. A Tragi-Comedy. London: Henry Herringman, 1669. [1691.]

The Humorists; A Comedy. London: Henry Herringman, 1671. [1691.]

The Miser, A Comedy. London: Thomas Collins and John Ford, 1672. [1691.]

Epsom-Wells. A Comedy. London: Henry Herringman, 1673. [1676, 1693, 1704.]

The Tempest, or The Enchanted Island. A Comedy. London: Henry Herringman, 1674. [1676, 1690, c. 1692, 1695, 1701.]

Psyche: A Tragedy. London: Henry Herringman, 1675. [1690.]

The Libertine: A Tragedy. London: Henry Herringman, 1676. [1692, 1697, 1704, 1705.]

The Virtuoso. A Comedy. London: Henry Herringman, 1676. [1691, 1704.]

The History of Timon of Athens, The Man-Hater. London: Henry Herringman, 1678. [1688, 1696, 1703.]

A True Widow. A Comedy. London: Benjamin Tooke, 1679.

The Woman-Captain: A Comedy. London: Samuel Carr, 1680.

The Lancashire Witches, and Tegue O Divelly The Irish Priest: A Comedy. London: John Starkey, 1682. [1691.]

The Medal of John Bayes: A Satyr Against Folly and Knavery. London: Richard Janeway, 1682.

Some Reflections Upon the Pretended Parallel in the Play Called The Duke of Guise. London: Francis Smith, 1683.

The Tenth Satyr of Juvenal, English and Latin. London: Gabriel Collins, 1687.

Selected Bibliography

The Squire of Alsatia. A Comedy. London: James Knapton, 1688. [1692, 1699.]

A Congratulatory Poem on His Highness the Prince of Orange His Coming into England. London: James Knapton, 1689.

A Congratulatory Poem To the Most Illustrious Queen Mary Upon Her Arrival in England. London: James Knapton, 1689.

Bury-Fair. A Comedy. London: James Knapton, 1689.

The Amorous Bigotte: With the Second Part of Tegue O Divelly. A Comedy. London: James Knapton, 1690. [1691.]

Ode on the Anniversary of the King's Birth. London: James Knapton, 1690.

The Scowrers. A Comedy. London: James Knapton, 1691.

Votum Perenne. A Poem to the King on New-Years-Day. London: Samuel Crouch, 1692.

The Volunteers, or The Stock-Jobbers. A Comedy. London: James Knapton, 1693.

The Works of Tho. Shadwell, Esq. London: James Knapton, 1693. [Collection of seventeen plays in one volume, omitting *The Tempest.*]

The Dramatick Works of Thomas Shadwell, Esq. 4 vols. London: J. Knapton and J. Tonson, 1720.

Thomas Shadwell (Mermaid Series). Ed. George Saintsbury. London: T. Fisher Unwin, n. d. [*Sullen Lovers, True Widow, Squire of Alsatia, Bury-Fair.*]

The Complete Works of Thomas Shadwell. Ed. Montague Summers. 5 vols. London: The Fortune Press, 1927.

Epsom-Wells and The Volunteers or The Stock-Jobbers. Ed. D. M. Walmsley. Boston: D. C. Heath and Company, 1930.

The Libertine, in *The Theatre of Don Juan: A Collection of Plays and Views, 1630-1963.* Ed. Oscar Mandel. Lincoln: University of Nebraska Press, 1963.

SECONDARY SOURCES

Omitted from this bibliography are some brief items which treat of sources or minute biographical facts. The number of long works on Shadwell being so few, I include several studies of Restoration comedy which consider him briefly or intermittently, and also, with some hesitation, eight dissertations published in Germany and Switzerland between 1887 and 1907. Although they shed some light on sources, they often contain information that is inaccurate or misleading.

ALLEMAN, GELLERT SPENCER. *Matrimonial Law and the Materials of Restoration Comedy.* Wallingford, Pennsylvania: no publisher, 1942. Excellent background material on civil and ecclesiastical marriage laws during the Restoration, with occasional illustrations from Shadwell's comedies.

AMMANN, ERNST. *Analysis of Thomas Shadwell's Lancashire Witches and Tegue O'Divelly the Irish Priest.* Bern: Gustav Grunau, 1905. Lauds Shadwell's democratic attitudes which he likens to those of modern times.

BEBER, OSCAR. *Thom. Shadwell's Bearbeitung des Shakespeare'schen "Timon of Athens."* Rostock: Carl Hinstorffs, 1897. On the adaptation of Shakespeare's tragedy.

BERNBAUM, ERNEST. *The Drama of Sensibility: A Sketch of the History of English Sentimental Comedy and Domestic Tragedy, 1696-1780.* Cambridge: Harvard University Press, 1925. Useful in considering certain sentimental tendencies in Shadwell who is briefly discussed in the early chapters.

BORGMAN, ALBERT S. *Thomas Shadwell: His Life and Comedies.* New York: New York University Press, 1928. Together with Summers' "Introduction" to the *Works,* this is the most important study of Shadwell's career and comedies.

CRULL, FRANZ. *Thomas Shadwell's (John Ozell's) und Henry Fielding's Comoedien "The Miser" in ihrem Verhältnis unter einander und zu ihrer gemeinsamen Quelle.* Rostock: Adler's Erben, 1899. English adaptations of *L'Avare* discussed in relation to their source.

ELWIN, MALCOLM. *The Playgoer's Handbook to Restoration Drama.* London: Jonathan Cape, 1928. Like other surveys of the drama of the period, this one treats Shadwell briefly.

ERICHSEN, ASMUS. *Thomas Shadwell's Komödie "The Sullen Lovers" in ihrem Verhältnis zu Molière's Komödien "Le Misanthrope" und "Les Fâcheux."* Flensburg: J. B. Meyer, 1906. French sources of Shadwell's first comedy closely discussed.

FUJIMURA, THOMAS H. *The Restoration Comedy of Wit.* Princeton: Princeton University Press, 1952. Studies the intellectual-esthetic basis of comedies by Shadwell's contemporaries.

GAGEN, JEAN ELIZABETH. *The New Woman: Her Emergence in English Drama, 1660-1730.* New York: Twayne Publishers, 1954. Considers several of Shadwell's heroines in her general discussion.

HARRIS, BRICE. *Charles Sackville, Sixth Earl of Dorset, Patron and Poet of the Restoration.* Urbana: University of Illinois Press, 1940. Together with similar studies on Newcastle and Sedley by Perry and Pinto, it offers glimpses of Shadwell's relationships with his patrons.

Selected Bibliography

UNDERWOOD, DALE. *Etherege and the Seventeenth-Century Comedy of Manners.* New Haven: Yale University Press, 1957. Illuminating background material for understanding Shadwell's management of popular contemporary philosophic attitudes.

WARD, ADOLPHUS WILLIAM. *A History of English Dramatic Literature to the Death of Queen Anne.* Vol. III. London: Macmillan and Company, Limited, 1899. Includes an often useful discussion of Shadwell.

WILCOX, JOHN. *The Relation of Molière to Restoration Comedy.* New York: Columbia University Press, 1938. Like Miles, considers Shadwell in the broader context of the dramatic activities of the age.

WILEY, AUTREY NELL. Editor. *Rare Prologues and Epilogues, 1642-1700.* London: George Allen and Unwin Limited, 1940. Reprints "A Lenten Prologue"; discusses it in relation to Shadwell's life and works.

Index

Index